king Sense of the Unfeasible

I dedicate this book to my dear mother Paula,
whose infinite love, strength and guidance
will remain with me forever.

Making Sense of the Unfeasible

My Life Journey with Asperger Syndrome

Marc Fleisher

Jessica Kingsley Publishers
London and New York

First published in the United Kingdom in 2003
by Jessica Kingsley Publishers Ltd
116 Pentonville Road
London N1 9JB, England
and
29 West 35th Street, 10th fl.
New York, NY 10001-2299, USA

www.jkp.com

Copyright © 2003 Marc Fleisher

Library of Congress Cataloging in Publication Data
A CIP catalog record for this book is available from the Library of Congress

British Library Cataloguing in Publication Data
A CIP catalogue record for this book is available from the British Library

ISBN 1 84310 165 3

Printed and Bound in Great Britain by
Athenaeum Press, Gateshead, Tyne and Wear

Contents

Acknowledgements

Many thanks to the following people, who have kindly allowed me to include them in my autobiography, or have helped in its production: my Dad, Maurice Fleisher, my sister, Po-Ling; Sid (Dad's cousin), his wife Doreen, and Ian; Monty and his wife Lorna; Peter and his wife Renate; my cousins Nicola, Sally and Katie; Sheila Coates; Pavanne; Rowena, Lesley and Helen (all at Brunel University Library); Ann Wilkes, Rebekah Spicer, Vivien Izzard and Beverley Williams (all at Brunel University); Eva Williams; Christine Hatfield; Kathy Erangey; Lesley Hatton; Margaret Shapley; Freda Higley; Daphne Fawcett; Pamela Yates; Rebecca and Simon Fraser; Ruth Smith; Marlies Kopp; and Rosemary West.

Introduction

Why did you pick up this book to read, I wonder? Perhaps you heard from a friend or family member that there was a new publication on Autism and its mysteries. Or maybe you were just curious about the title and thought you'd glance inside. Whatever your reason, the fact is that you are now here, reading the first page. I'm very glad you are, because I would like to tell you about an incredible journey I have made. A journey with bold and ambitious objectives. A journey that stirs the mind! A voyage that will take you to the limit of your imagination and beyond. One that may just change your life!

I hope it will! I hope that by the time you have finished reading this book, you will have a much clearer picture of what Autism is about. You will be more tolerant of Autistic people's sometimes repetitive behaviour and excessive worries, and will understand to a greater extent why these worries take place. You will appreciate the urgent need for the right sort of support to be available to all sufferers. You will tell your friends and family of your new-found knowledge. And ultimately, when your friends tell their friends, and they tell their friends, an incredible transformation will have happened across the country. Autism will be universally known. Our fear of the unknown will have been conquered.

The lives of thousands of Autistic people will change, from isolated helpless figures in mental institutions to confident people with jobs, social lives, good future prospects and above all, respect from the community as a whole. I will show, to a largely disbelieving world, that in my journey as an autistic man I was able to break the vicious circle of withdrawing into my own no-hope, make-believe world, and with the right sort of professional help have been able to achieve goals beyond my wildest dreams. We cannot deny any other Autistic person this right, for if I can do these things, other people can too. That is my journey's boldest quest. To give them that right. And this is my story.

Before we embark on my own epic life-story, let us clear up a few more general points. First the obvious question, and the one that people have been asking me for years – exactly what is Autism? In some people's minds the term conjures up visions of someone like in the film *Rainman*, incredibly gifted academically in the sciences, but socially in the Dark Ages. Other people have visions of mentally retarded individuals confined to special homes, totally dependent on others, with seemingly no prospect of improvement. Still other people have never even heard the term. Can we clarify the situation? It's tough!

There is no one right answer to this question. Like the common cold, there are so many severities and variations that even the experts are sometimes baffled. We could very loosely describe Autism as a social and communication disorder, but this draws no fine lines with many other disabilities that can be present. Thus the condition is much more subtle and harder to recognise (and therefore arguably worse) than someone with an obvious disability, such as being confined to a wheelchair. This is not to say, of course, that other disabled people do not suffer, but at least their disabilities can be seen in respect to help being readily available. The fact that Autistic people can appear normal in their external appearance can make the problem far worse, since to an outsider they can simply appear badly behaved. Thus, it makes people forget that while they can do so courageously well in some areas, they are struggling to do the everyday things that most of us take for granted.

You might be wondering at this point what type of 'everyday things' I'm referring to. Let me give you a great example – one that actually happened to me. Once when I was a bit younger (but still an adult) I went to a pub on a day out with a friend who offered to buy me a drink. He didn't say so in as many words, but simply said, 'Drinks on the house, mate!' I was utterly bewildered! I had no concept of this so-called social idiosyncrasy and for the next hour or two I kept wondering why on earth they would put a drink on the roof of the pub! Would they use a ladder? How would they balance it up there if the roof was sloping? And surely if it rained, the drink would be ruined. It wasn't until later that day, after the whole room had burst out laughing about my apparent misconception that I found out the true meaning of the phrase.

The bottom line of this discussion is that most Autistic people take things very *literally*. They are unable to distinguish between serious conversations and the numerous so-called light-hearted remarks that occur every day requiring that special social 'know-how' to be able to pick up hints. This can be especially hurtful for those affected individuals towards the more able range of the Autistic spectrum, who have managed to establish some social skills, but are obvious targets to be taken advantage of, and additionally can often cause embarrassment without meaning to. It often results in Autistic people finding it hard to trust others, and/or withdrawing and becoming over-shy about meeting new people.

It can simply be the fear of the unknown – that something might go wrong that will stop Autistic people from exposing themselves to unfamiliar situations, long before anything does actually go wrong. And the more they avoid society the worse the feelings of isolation become. To get an idea of what these feelings are, imagine that you are somehow marooned on a small island in the middle of the Pacific Ocean. It is an island with plenty of vegetables, with plenty of fruits and water to live on, a safe cave for a shelter, but no other people on the island. You have a two-way radio with which you can talk to your family, who are based in America, as often as you wish but you are never allowed to leave the island. Few people could stand this set-up for long, yet Autistic people could feel like this for years without proper treatment.

Another important factor that is often overlooked by the general population is the depth of feeling of the Autistic person when faced with uncertain or stressful situations. Let us imagine a particular theoretical situation: picture a father and his Autistic son in the dining room of their average-sized house. The father is busy writing a letter for his home business, but he has promised to take his son for a walk in the park in a few minutes. On his workdesk, amongst the usual types of accessories, is a holder for a set of pens and an average-sized wooden school ruler that Dad has kept since his heyday, placed in the middle of the desk.

'Come on!' says the son. 'I want to go out.'

'I won't be long,' Dad replies, turning around slightly, 'I just want to finish this letter.' Dad then turns back and leans his right arm over the table to pick up a different colour pen from the holder. As he does so, his right elbow gently and innocently brushes against the ruler so that it is no longer on the desk top centre, but only just balancing on the edge. With no further jolts the ruler will probably remain, but any further movement or gust of wind and it is likely to fall, making a loud clatter on the hard stone floor. At this instant the Autistic son's life, from his point of view, has turned into a nightmare. The whole room seems to dim apart from the ruler which seems brightly lit. Many Autistic people are very susceptible to noise and will do almost anything to avoid it – the noise, say, of a ruler clanging onto the stone floor. The ruler! The ruler! Nothing else matters. The son has a desperately urgent mission – he must get to the ruler. In three quick strides, heart beating, body sweating and panic breathing, he is there, pushing the ruler back to the table's centre. He made it! Safety. The ruler will no longer fall. Extreme worry, now intense relief. Just how intense? We shall see.

'Don't say you're worrying about a stupid ruler, son? Whatever next?' Dad says, rising from his chair. 'Are you ready for that walk?' Just then the telephone rings and Dad steps to answer it. As he lifts the receiver he is smiling and carefree, but in a few short seconds this all changes. The smile disappears, he starts to shake, and tears well up in his eyes. It is now Dad's turn for life to become a nightmare! It is the police. There has been a terrible accident. The only other family member, their daughter, has been thrown out of a car by the seaside, on her holiday 100 miles away from home. She is clinging onto the top of a tall cliff with one hand, her other hand is broken. And there is a 1000-foot drop onto jagged rocks if she falls. To make matters even worse, the accident and emergency rescue people are on strike in that county, so it's up to Dad to jump into his car and go and rescue her!

What sort of thoughts are going through Dad's mind as he climbs into his car? His daughter cannot hold on for ever. At any moment she may be forced to let go. And how many moments are there in a 100-mile drive? 'Feelings of utter dread' is an understatement. Now imagine the relief, the joy, and the unbounded happiness if Dad does get to the cliff in time, and pulls his daughter to safety. Now this is where we get to the good part. I asked you how much the Autistic son was worrying about that ruler falling on the stone floor and making a noise. Well, I'll tell you. He was just as worried as Dad was when he got that phone call! All the agony, all the dread, exactly the same intensity. And the relief felt when that ruler was pushed back on the table was every bit as great as when Dad managed to save his daughter! This fact may be hard to grasp for many people – this is what this condition can do to some of us.

I have described above an example of what I call the 'life/death comparison'. For all those parents out there, the next time your Autistic son or daughter makes a comment about something that appears to be totally trivial, it is worth considering for a moment this comparison – consider the depth of what their anxiety might be. It should be stressed that not all Autistic people worry as acutely as this. Often, with the right sort of help many phobias can be overcome before they reach crisis point. But the condition does exist. It's not always easy to keep your temper when your child is clearly driving you mad. The task of coping with things day after day should not be done alone in any case. It is too big a job for parents to expect to do all on their own. That is why professional help must be sought (more on this in the later chapters).

But it's all very well saying 'seek professional help for the Autistic person'. Many parents would be extremely glad to even be in this position, in recognising that Autism is the problem that needs to be solved. We first need to 'recognise' the Autism. This can be a very difficult thing to do. If noticing someone in a wheelchair could be compared to noticing a flat tyre on your car, or locating a road on our local town map, then noticing the symptoms of Autism will be like knowing what is wrong with your car when it just won't start because of some internal malfunction, or of trying to find a road in your local town from a large-scale map of England with only the A roads shown. Parents should always trust their gut-feeling about their child's behaviour – after all, they've lived with him all their lives. Most important, if they suspect Autism, they should seek out help from people who specifically know about the condition. Seeking advice from people without this background knowledge could be disastrous (see Chapter 1).

Given the critical importance of recognising the condition of Autism in the first place, what are the tell-tale signs to look for? At an early age, most normal children are able to attract their parents' attention to something that has caught their interest, even if they don't know the right words; for example, a child seeing a plane in the sky for the first time would be likely to point at it and make a sound, to which the normal reaction from the parent will be: 'That is an aeroplane!' It is through this development that the child can pick up and develop knowledge on an ever-increasing vocabulary of words. In sharp contrast, the Autistic child is far more likely not to point at such an object, and indeed will fail to make any sound at all, resulting in the parent not being given the opportunity to voice words. Thus the ability of the child to develop new words and knowledge is severely impaired. In addition, from about 14 months of age many Autistic people have a lack of any imaginative play routine such as playing with a toy train and making a 'choo-choo' sound, or having any concept of what the object really is. They also often lack ability to copy actions or instructions from their parents when being asked to 'mouth' new words, etc.

Most parents will of course be aware that there is always that certain inquisitive age where speech has been mastered, at least partially, and every other minute the questions keep coming: 'Dad, what is this?' 'Mum, what is this food, and why is it this colour?' 'Dad, what are houses made out of?' This may no doubt get very tiring at times, but it is an important process of learning for the child. Many bits of knowledge assembled during this period can be stored in the long-term memory for life. In contrast the Autistic child will generally ask very few questions, or even none. Consequently, the chance to assemble knowledge is once again reduced, and the affected child will often withdraw into his 'own world' of phobias and perhaps stereotype and repetitive behaviour. In order to make progress, it is vital that the gap between the fantasies and the real world is bridged, at least partially, and communication is the vital key here. Sign language and computerised methods of talking should be considered if verbal speech is absent or very small. Without this the child will have no means of revealing his frustrations to the real world and his parents, and will 'bottle things up' in a vicious circle.

Details of methods of communication and how to apply them to the Autistic person should be sought out from authorities with specific knowledge and training in the condition. The difficulties that Autistic people have in developing their language skills is also self-evident because from an early age most show no interest in mixing with other children, for example at school, and will tend to remain by themselves, making them an obvious target for bullies. The medical aspects as to what actually causes Autism are very complex, and believed to be associated with an inability of certain parts of the brain to function normally. It is not my intention to discuss this in any great depth, since a number of texts have been produced, and interested people should refer to these. It is my opinion that there are a number of questions that cannot be answered by a medical journal, such as the mental feelings within the condition. As someone affected, rather than a non-Autistic author, I liken this to trying to judge a book by its cover alone. It is on these questions that I hope to concentrate most of my book.

An important point must be made before we progress. I shall be referring to myself as an Autistic man throughout the text, and in the most general sense this is correct. However, I wish to make it clear that I actually suffer from a specific form of Autism known as Asperger Syndrome (AS). At the more able end of the full variety of Autistic characteristics, the phrase is often, although incorrectly, assumed to be a more mild version of general Autism. In fact it is merely a specialised form of the condition which can in its own way be just as devastating a handicap as any other form of Autism. I shall attempt to clarify the situation briefly, but interested readers who wish to know the precise medical differences between the two should consult the diagnostic manuals, the most recent currently being the *Diagnostic and Statistical Manual of Mental Disorders IV* (Washington, DC: American Pyschiatric Association, 1994).

It is certainly true that the three core difficulties experienced by Autistic people in general are also present in Asperger individuals. These difficulties are:

1.   Problems understanding social language (as in our drink on the roof example).

2.   An inability to know what is socially acceptable (for instance, not to stick out your tongue in public).

3.   Difficulties in relationships.

However, people with AS tend to be more verbal and have a pretty good grasp of literal vocabulary, and additionally will often have particular interests of a specific nature such as the study of the sciences. The fact that many of these individuals attempt to form relationships, which then run into problems when the partner has not understood the special needs of the sufferer, is in its own way even harder for the affected one than for the more general Autistic person, who perhaps was never able to form a friendship in the first place and thus was spared the pain of rejection.

It is nearly time to begin our journey though my life-story: a journey which is to end with two Maths degrees, several public appearances on national TV, giving talks on Autism up to international level all across the country, and a genuine passionate desire to help others through teaching, and increasing the awareness of the general population that 'from this day forward' a new age has sprung. The difficulties and restrictions of Autism can be overcome – it has been proved. I have been talking quite generally so far, and in Appendix 1 of this book I shall do so again. I shall ask how in a material sense we can actually set about making this transformation. There are things that every parent of a sufferer, no matter how bad, can do to set this change in process. But for now, you might ask, how were all these achievements possible? Behind every one of my major achievements is a long list of smaller ones, which had to be mastered step by step. And behind every one of those was required a great deal of sacrifice, pain, planning and willpower. Let us delay no longer! Sit down in a comfortable chair, get yourself settled, and strap yourself in if you're the jumpy type! Let's go!

CHAPTER 1

The Early Years

Years 0–9

The human heartbeat! There are few things more natural and yet fundamentally essential for the existence of all individuals. It was the repeating beats of my Mum's heart that were my first memory. And her breathing. I was aware of my surroundings – I could see shapes, mainly red, but different shades of red. The darkest shades were almost black, the lightest shades almost yellow. The shapes seemed to move left and right at times, at other times there was almost no movement. And the speed of the heartbeats and the breathing seemed to vary, sometimes slow, sometimes quicker, once or twice very quickly. At these later times I was aware of certain jolts or bumps. I could also hear sounds like mumbled voices. Could this be that I was aware of things while still inside my mother, experiencing her 'rest' times with slower heartbeat and active times with a quicker one? Or could the ravages of time have blurred my memory so that these are only echoes of dreams or sightings in my young life after I was born? To this day I am undecided. Perhaps this is destined to stay a mystery, one of the deep unexplainables of all human lives.

This much is known. At about 5pm on 3 May 1967, I, Marc Reuben Fleisher, was born in Bury St Edmunds, Suffolk, with one older sister, Tanya (about two and a half), and my Mum Paula (about

30) , and Dad Maurice (about 35). In the first few years there were no abnormalities, at least none acutely visible to the rest of my family, to suggest I was to have a medical disability label. Yet in my mind something deep down told me I was never destined to be quite like most other people. But in the innocence of youth, when one day seems like an eternity, slow development can be forgiven. It was only later, much later, when the normal child is expected to develop that my differences became infinitely more marked. Up to the age of four, it was largely in my mind alone that I was somehow different.

My family tree was quite a large one, but partly due to my lack of ability or interest in socialising at an early age I only really got to know a few of my immediate relations well. Among them was my Mum's brother, Peter, and his wife Renate, who was born in Germany. They were known to me as Uncle Peter and Aunty Renate, and we used to go and visit them from time to time at their home in Beaconsfield. They had three daughters, Nicola, Sally and Katie, all of whom worked at Heathrow at one point. Peter himself had had an active past serving in the merchant navy, followed by a job in the building trade. In my early childhood he was running a newsagent's in Beaconsfield quite close to his home, while later he went on to run a tea shop within a large store.

On the other side of the family, my Dad had a cousin called Sid who was a printer. His wife was called Doreen. These two were probably best thought of as second cousins to me. The interesting fact about them was that they had a child called Ian who was also known to be Autistic. It is a strange fact that there are about four times as many males who are Autistic as there are females. In my early years often I made no distinction between times when the whole family was present and when they were not. I would much rather go and play with my toy train and track set, for example, instead of sitting and talking with the others. My Dad also had another cousin called Monty and wife Lorna. It wasn't until much later in life that I became more aware of the importance of family relations and how they fit into the overall structure of a person's past.

We lived in an average-sized, four-bedroom house in Pakenham, a small village only a few miles away from the town of Bury St

Edmunds. From an early age I seemed able to picture scenes and properties of this house and the surrounding neighbourhood. Our house,
for example, was one of three close but detached neighbouring
houses, each of which had one very large tree at the bottom of its
garden. Our own tree was a giant horse chestnut, which had one of its
branches hanging quite low down over the roadway at the bottom of
the gardens. My sister and I used to watch every time a double-decker
bus drove past. It would hit the branch, and we always wondered if it
would be knocked off. The big tree next door was an ash, which
always came into leaf later than any other tree I knew (about
mid-June). At the bottom of our back garden there was a playing field
with some swings in it, and farmland lay beyond this. The images of
these things, characteristics of the landscape, and countless others,
have been kept deep within my mind, like a photographic memory – a
rapid succession of slides, each showing a key moment or place in my
early life.

Of course I had many of the experiences that any normal child
might expect to encounter in the first five years. Falling off my bike
into the nettles, this was a bad day. Celebrating Christmas, this was a
good day. I also had dreams that any young boy might have; for
example, I used to dream I could fly. But there were also other dreams,
perhaps less normal. Two of these stand out. The first probably stems
from the fact that in my bedroom I had a light almost above my bed
with a light-shade that was rather loose. I used to imagine that this
light-shade would fall on top of my face, and get stuck there. I then
had to say the continuous sound 'eeeee' for perhaps an hour, sometimes less, sometimes more, until the light-shade had mercy on me and
let me run to the rest of the family. And while I was stuck with the
light-shade, although I could hear other people's voices, I had this
overwhelming feeling of helplessness, that I was in a situation beyond
my control. I'm not sure where the 'eeeee' sound stemmed from,
although it could have been from a tree, since a tree was visible outside
my bedroom window, so maybe that got stuck in my memory.

The second nasty dream was even more frightening. It involved
the chimney of our house (and other houses) having magic powers. I

would only be safe if I was inside the house with all the windows shut – otherwise I would be lifted up through the air and end up stuck on the chimney-pot, having to say the word 'Tuf!' repeatedly. This word might have stemmed from 'tough object', for a chimney-pot is generally strong and can withstand most (if not all!) the elements. Although being shut up in the house might have left me vulnerable to 'eeeing' the light, this was infinitely preferable to 'Tufing' the chimney, because the light usually had mercy on me at some point, and I was never stuck under the light-shade for more than half a day. Indeed I sometimes bargained, saying to the light-shade, 'If I eeeee you for two hours this morning, can I be with Mum for the rest of the day?' To which the light-shade would agree. In sharp contrast, if the chimney caught me, I really would be stuck on the roof for ever and ever – the chimney never had any mercy. I even dreamt I had to stay on the chimney-pot when there was a fire in the house and smoke coming out, so that I was coughing as well as saying the word 'Tuf'.

Once I had a particularly vivid episode of this latter dream. I was walking back to our house after a day out with Mum, Dad and Tanya when I suddenly felt myself being lifted up through the air towards the chimney-pot. I screamed 'No!' and in desperation held hands with my sister and Mum and Dad, trying to keep on the ground. Eventually the pull of the chimney was too strong and one by one I had to let go of the other family members. I felt numb, helpless and terribly afraid, afraid of a dread that would never go away. My family just stood and watched, unable to help. Of course these were just childhood dreams, and yet I believe there is a deeper significance to them in my life in general. I feel that almost subconsciously during my first five years I was aware that I was different from other people; that I had problems that other people couldn't understand, and could end up watching others live normal lives with me being alone with my phobias. I also felt that the worries would last for ever. The eternity of my time spent on an imaginary chimney-pot could be seen as a virtual parallel to the fact that Autism is a life-long condition, although of course at that time I don't think any of our family (or most of the world in the early

1970s) understood the term. Most of the detailed research has been done only recently.

I attended nursery school for a period when I was about four years old where I used to like playing with the various toys there on my own, but had no interest in talking to any of the other children. I did get upset after a while, however, when one child called Ros Poz used to try to keep every toy. My social difficulties plus my unusual phobias as a youngster had so far not been significantly noticed, but this was about to change when I turned five. On one side of our home there was a large collection of small trees and shrubs, and on the other side of this was a primary school – very convenient in terms of walking there, for it was here that I started attending school full time. For the first time I was in an environment where most children would be expected to start at least some correspondence with others. It was about this period that my apparent inability to mix caught the attention of my Mum, who realised something was not quite right. In addition there were also other little incidents that were making me stand out.

One day, on a long and hot summer afternoon, my teacher was sitting outside the school buildings in the cool shade of the big oak tree with the class, reading the famous story of 'Icarus the bird', which as legend has it flew too close to the sun so that his feathers started to burn off. Right in the middle of this story the teacher was suddenly interrupted by a loud voice from one of her listeners, remarking, 'STOP! STOP! DON'T BOTHER READING THIS ANY MORE! THIS INFORMATION IS STUPID! HOW COULD A BIRD FLY ANYWHERE NEAR THE SUN? NOT ONLY IS THERE A TOTAL LACK OF OXYGEN IN OUTER SPACE, BUT BY THE TIME THIS BIRD GOT ABOVE THE TROPOSPHERE IT WOULD HAVE FROZEN TO DEATH!' The teacher looked dumbstruck! Then she looked rather annoyed, saying, 'Be quiet, no talking when I'm speaking please.' Now that voice was mine, and unknown to the teacher I had been reading a book on the levels of the atmosphere beforehand, and had memorised every single detail. Even at this early age I had a great love of astronomy and mathematics, could count in the thousands easily, and now was expressing what I had learnt.

This incident illustrates not one but two important concepts of the Autistic child. On the one hand my incredible factual knowledge and ability to remember facts was taking lots of people by surprise. On the other hand I did not have the social sense to wait until the end of the story before expressing my views. The point is that I had taken everything literally, and was unable to distinguish between fact and fiction. I was also unable to sort many physical aspects of everyday living unless I had been shown exactly. A good example of this is when my Mum showed me one morning how to tie up my shoelaces. Later my Mum had to go out for the rest of the morning and while she had gone I felt the urge to go out in the garden. Sure enough, I remembered how to tie my shoelaces up to go out...but...when I came back in the house there I was, stuck in my shoes for the whole morning getting blisters, because I had not been shown how to untie the shoelaces. I was not able to relate this to tying them up in reverse.

In response to her growing realisation of my oddities, when I was about five my Mum took me to seek advice, from a young inexperienced doctor who had no understanding of Autism at all. This was to turn out to be a grave mistake for it ended up with the doctor calling me mentally retarded, something which my Mum was so upset about she never really got over it. And there was very little she could do in the few years that followed, for the condition was just not understood well enough. All she had was her faith that I was clearly not that bad, was very talented in some areas, but just had strange phobias and fixations in others. There are few things that are worse for a mother than having something wrong with your child but not knowing what it is, for in this case you do not know how to help. How she coped with these early years I don't know. All I will say is that she was a very strong person.

There were one or two additional and unusual features that my parents were noticing. I was developing a strange restricted diet, having no milk, eggs, vegetables and a host of other foods that a growing child would expect to be having. The only meat I ate was sausages, and I only accepted them if they were a particular type of small sausage (Bowes). Anything else in the way of a sausage I refused to eat! I loved peanuts as well, and I got my protein from both these foods. I ate cereals, bread and Marmite, some chocolate, and crisps and chips for carbohydrates, but very little else. And so it went on, year after year, with my only main cooked meal being sausages and chips – 365 days a year, including Christmas Day and New Year's Day! This extraordinary feat surprised my family. For most people, eating other meat and food as well, this would be a very unhealthy diet. And yet I appeared to latch on to the food and seemed healthy. I was told slightly later in life that the reason for this is that my body has a strange metabolism (the doctor's verdict) and that I was somehow obtaining most of the nutrients I needed.

The restricted diet syndrome is in fact a characteristic of many Autistic people, who discover certain types of food they like and then want to stick with them, not changing for anything else. I had no desire to try other foods. Even the thought of anything else, especially items not solid such as mashed potato, made me feel sick. One day my Mum had to go out and it was left to my Dad to do the cooking. As she left, Mum said to Dad 'Don't forget to put the potatoes on for Marc', meaning the potatoes were to be peeled and then cooked as chips. But Dad had misunderstood, for both he and Tanya were having mashed potato that day, and it was thought I had decided to try some as well. When they dished up the food I was horrified, and promptly burst into tears! I was made to at least try a bit because it was now cooked, and was physically sick as a result. Yet my Dad only wanted what was best for me. Any ordinary naughty youngsters might try to refuse food they didn't like if they thought they could get away with it, and this would not be for their own good. At the time I could not have expected any more understanding because my condition was not known by the family.

It was my sister who provided a vital separation from my feelings of isolation in not being able to make other friends. She was the only person of roughly my own age to whom I could relate. We played countless games, both inside and out. We had two trees, standing side by side in the shrubbery between our house and the school, which we used to climb. One was Tan's tree, the other mine. Of course, being slightly older than me, Tan did have certain rights (seemingly!). For example, she was *always* allowed to sit in the front seat of the car wherever we went on a journey by road, which was a little pet hate of mine at the time. But overall I can honestly say that the only happy times I ever spent with someone else of a similar age during this period were the times with my sister. My Dad was working in the video production industry full time, and my Mum also had a number of part-time jobs including working in a local sweet shop, so inevitably there were many occasions when I had to play on my own. (My sister was perhaps busy or occupied with other friends, because she could make friends from an early age, and frequently did.)

It was in these times on my own that I first discovered something I loved doing in the process of playing. This was to mimic events in the real world, chiefly the natural or prehistoric world, because I had no concept at this stage of how humans operated a modern technical society. For example, if I was splashing lots of water in the bath, and spilt some on the floor, I would make a big noise, imagining that a huge tidal wave had just occurred somewhere on earth, perhaps in the Pacific Ocean. I had read about dinosaurs, and if I knocked my toys over it would be as if a huge dinosaur had knocked some trees down 100 million years ago, in some prehistoric swamp. If I fell over and hurt myself, or had an accident and hurt my knee, etc., I would parallel this with a more serious event in the world, such as the possible asteroid hitting the earth and wiping out the dinosaurs. For just as this had a far greater effect on all types of life-form 65 million years ago, so I would never forget when I hurt my knee, and even years later be wary of slippery icy surfaces!

The process by which I was comparing my actions with other events had a far deeper significance than just childhood fantasies. As we shall see, this was just the mere splattering, less than 1 per cent of 1 per cent of what was to come in later years – all shall be revealed! But at this point the key principle of evading responsibility should be known. It was almost as if I was afraid of the responsibilities of my actions, and wished instead to think of it being an event or happening elsewhere, thus avoiding blame. It may have been a deep-rooted subconscious fear of looking stupid, or looking the fool, having already been teased on numerous occasions at school. I developed a fixation with time, and when I got kept in after school one day for an extra half an hour because I was stuck on some homework, I was upset for weeks afterwards, fearing the same thing would happen again.

When I was about eight I left the primary school next door and started attending a rather bigger school in Ixworth, a large village about two or three miles away from us. This involved catching a school bus each morning, and as we were the last stop on the route before the school it was nearly always fairly full up. I used to hate it when I had to stand up, since any jolt on the bus would mean I would nearly fall over, or knock into someone, and often the children would call out or laugh to see me trip up. It ended up with me turning up at the bus stop about 45 minutes early, just to get in the front of the queue to get a seat. With this worry getting out of proportion, I often braved the elements and stood out in the pouring rain, or snow.

We have had a brief insight into my early life, a life with the loving care of my parents, my sister for company, and a life with many happy memories; maybe one with strange behavioural patterns in me on occasions, but in the innocence of youth these could perhaps be forgiven. After all, so long as the family stuck together surely these phobias couldn't get the better of us. This may have been awkward at times, but they were about to get infinitely worse. A chance event, totally unpredicted and without any warning, would make certain of this. My world and the state of my family were soon to be changed for ever. In order to discover why, we shall have to enter the next phase of my life story, from the age of 10 to 13, which was one of the most traumatic and yet also most crucial periods of my existence.

CHAPTER 2

Crisis Time

Years 10–13

W hen I was ten years old, my life in Suffolk came to an end as we moved house to Berkshire to a place in Barkham Ride (near Wokingham). This was a result of my Dad getting a new job, still in the video and TV industry, but in a new area. We had not been there long before one of my sister's dreams came true – she owned a horse for the first time, called Pepper. Tanya had always loved horses and riding and had always wanted to own one. My first impressions of the new home were not that good however, even if it was similar in size to our previous one. I sensed it somehow felt unlucky, dark, almost spooky, as if our family should not have moved, and that a dark period for everyone was on the horizon. As we shall see, almost like a sixth sense (a premonition) these fears were not unfounded.

The family had all been working quite hard with the move and my parents felt we needed a break, so they set up a holiday in southern France for us. We had been on holidays in England before but this was the first time of going abroad, and we all looked forward to the hot weather expected. On 13 May 1978 the journey began. We had already crossed the Channel, had just eaten in a service station close by, and now started the long drive down through the country to nearly its southernmost tip where our holiday destination was. But we never got to our destination. Instead, something terrible happened, something that was to throw my already difficult passage through Autistic life into turmoil, and catapult it into one over a thousand times harder, and ensure that things would never be the same for our family again.

It all happened so quickly. One moment we were driving along talking and laughing. Then a burst tyre, the car swerving all over the road. We skidded towards the grass verge, which for most of its entirety along that stretch of road was just grass. But a stray bollard, a solid object sticking out of the ground which would not move, lay in our way. Instead of just stopping, our car therefore turned right over. The next thing I knew I was rolling over and over in the grass. Then I stopped rolling and felt the pain – terrible pain. I saw luggage and clothes and squashed food packets everywhere in the grass. I saw my Mum and Dad stagger out of the car, walking around dazed trying to pick things up. And my sister – I could not see her anywhere. Then I saw an ambulance that had come for us. In great pain I uttered the words, 'Ambulance. Hospital.' It was all that mattered, for us to get to a place that eased the pain. Other cars sped by, some slowed to have a look; one man even took a photo of us, maybe a reporter for a newspaper. Then I was inside the ambulance on the way to hospital.

But this was not a hospital I knew. It was a strange French hospital. I was for a while separated from the family and taken into a strange room with doctors touching and examining me with all sorts of instruments, to assess my injuries. The worst thing was the language. I had never learnt French. I asked to go to the bathroom. I asked for some water. I said, 'Where are my Mum and Dad?' But no one seemed to understand what I was saying. I had always compared having Autism as being like someone lost in a strange country with an unknown language and having to ask for help. Now this comparison was coming true, literally, in the extreme. Eventually, after what was probably not very long but seemed like an eternity, I was reunited with my Mum and Dad, who had got away with just minor scratches. I was hurt with serious although not life-threatening bruises, including near one of my eyes. For a couple of minutes I felt relief. As long as we were together we would somehow pull through. But then another thought – how badly hurt was my sister?

Then Mum and Dad told me. I would never see my sister again. She was thrown out of the car when it turned over. She never stood a chance. Doctors had tried to revive her in vain. 'But this can't be true,' I thought. It must be a nightmare. A nightmare that any minute I would wake up from. Our holiday plans now in ruins, we flew home to England in a private jet, where I spent a few days in a local hospital recovering from my bruises. Then one day shortly after, we drove home, where our ginger cat ran to greet us just as it always did. But there was a terrible numbness, emptiness, the whole family had simply not taken it all in yet. The terrible reality was that I had not only lost my dear sister, but also seemingly my only window on the outside world for communicating with someone of my own age. In the days and weeks that followed, with the tears, frustration and arguments as reality sank in, I was having to cope not only with my Autism, which can magnify greatly every slight anxiety, but also with the family grief that anyone would go through after an occurrence of this magnitude.

With my sister now gone, there was nothing to break the terrible feeling of isolation (that I had always felt to some extent) now running riot. I started retreating into my make-believe parallel world much more intensely, for a cloud hung over us in real life. So in my parallel world too, conditions were of death, mirroring the image of the great ice ages that occurred across northern Europe about 12,000 years ago. There were no plants, no vegetation, the sparkle and the flowers of life had gone. There was just coldness, darkness, and the terror of total isolation that can only be pictured if you imagined that you too were lost, not just somewhere on earth today, but in a time in the distant past where the only help you would ever find would be from primitive people living in caves.

Then, in the midst of all this sorrow, one day I had another vision, a premonition possibly. I told my parents about it. I saw that we would move house again, to make a fresh start. We would move into a four-bedroom house with a hall floor slightly raised, with steps going down to both the kitchen and the lounge. And just a few months later this incredibly came true, almost exactly as I had described. Our third home was in Booker, near the town of High Wycombe in Buckinghamshire. I can't know fully how I had these visions – they normally only happen when I am under a lot of stress. And this move was the start of a sequence of events that would lead to my Autism being recognised.

My schooling was in a total mess. I had changed schools about six or seven times after my sister's death. No one had known quite what was wrong with me, but I was being bullied and teased nearly all the time (on one occasion hiding nearly all day in the bathroom). This was about to change. When I was 11, our new local doctor in High Wycombe was listening to my parents' concern over me when he made a recommendation that we went to see a brilliant lady in London who was expert in recognising disabilities. This turned out to be a real turning point, as within five minutes of seeing me she had diagnosed me as Autistic. My parents had spent nearly my whole life wondering about my strange behavioural difficulties without really knowing where to turn. The relief that they felt at this moment was identical to the instant when our hypothetical Autistic boy pushed that ruler back onto his Dad's workdesk! Now at last they had found the key to an explanation for my many phobias. They had an understanding what my problems were. The next question however was what they could do about it. The lady who had diagnosed me then told us about a place in Chinnor, Oxfordshire, called the Chinnor Resource Unit for Autistic Children, at this time (1980) about the only one of its kind in the country. Even though the place was about ten miles away and in a different county, my parents decided to send me there. It was one of the best decisions they ever made.

The main idea of this unit, a small building next door to the normal primary school (St Andrew's, Chinnor), was to integrate affected pupils into the mainstream school next door (and later into local secondary schools, etc.), but always with the support and back-up of the unit staff who are all thoroughly trained in the condition. This support normally took the form of a member of staff 'sitting in' with the pupil in lesson times, but also included specific periods each week where the individual concerned spent time in the specialised unit, for help more intensively available than would normally be found in the main school. Examples of such help could be for shopping and cooking; for example, a group of us would be sent into the village to buy simple products such as margarine or butter used in cooking, learning how to use money in the process. We would then return to the unit and learn how to cook and prepare food using the items that we had bought. This would be a vital skill in later life. The unit's operation began in the early 1970s, so by the time I started attending (1980) there were already plenty of other pupils.

The vital ingredient here of course was that all the staff knew and had first-hand experience of Autism. In particular, whereas my parents had done everything for me, the unit staff challenged my ability to do things. I had to figure out problems using logical step-by-step arguments. On the other hand, if I ever really was stuck or got in a panic, whether in the classroom or with an activity in the unit itself, the staff would step in to rescue me, knowing that it is equally important not to push too hard or, as the saying goes, 'Don't run before you can walk.' Of course, often I did not appreciate this help at the time; after all I was still quite young and it just seemed like hard work. But subconsciously, deep down, this unique combination of specialised, trained help and support, along with periods in the mainstream school so as not to lose contact with other ordinary pupils, was worth its weight in gold.

For a start, I began making great strides in my academic work, as I felt I was working in a safer environment where people understood me. I had quite a few gaps in my knowledge as a result of my disrupted or missed schooling in previous years, but what I did know I knew well, and I was able to fill in many of those gaps quite quickly. Another particular form of help that stands out in my memory was a 'social skills' group run inside the unit once a week after lessons. In this group we were made to act out role play of situations that could happen to any one of us socially in real life. For example, suppose a stranger came up to you in the street and said, 'Your trousers are looking raggy – you really should dress better than that, you know.' How would you best handle it without causing an argument? Or suppose you found a sheep loose in the lane and a broken farm fence – who could you trust to help you? This was especially useful since many of us Autistic people had not had the chance to experience such events through socialising on our own, yet they would be memorised for later life.

The other pupils in the unit had the Autistic condition in various degrees of severity. Those worst affected could hardly talk at all, and any time spent in the mainstream school next door was either very limited or absent at that time, simply because they were not judged to be ready; first their confidence had to be built up through activities within the unit itself. However, there were many others, including myself, who were able to spend some time in the classroom, at first with a unit staff member always present. The best part I found however was that the more used to the class environment I got, and the more confident I became, this support could be slowly but surely withdrawn. Ultimately I was spending nearly all the time in mainstream classes on my own, safe in the knowledge that I could report straight back to the unit after the lesson if I had any worries.

The manifestations of my condition were still surfacing in unexpected ways. I had a fixation with time which was to lead to a major worry. My mother had been driving me to and from Chinnor for the first few weeks, but it was decided that as I was likely to be with this unit help for several years this was not practical. I would have to learn to catch the bus from Chinnor to High Wycombe. At first a member of staff always waited at the Chinnor bus stop until the bus came, but after a while I was made to wait on my own. This caused untold tears – it was all very well if the bus was on time (but how often does this happen these days?). If the bus was even one minute late I started to worry, by five minutes I would virtually be in a panic. I felt that if the bus did not come I would be stuck there at the bus stop all night, in a situation beyond my control. It was the same at the other end. My Mum always met me on the main West Wycombe Road to drive me up the Booker Hill on the last mile home. If she wasn't there, or even a couple of minutes late, I always feared the worst – that I would be stuck on the main road, or that she had had an accident, or that her car had broken down, once again a situation where I felt helpless.

As well as continuing to have excessive worries such as this, I still often mimicked events that had happened to me and imagined that they were in fact other events in my make-believe fantasy world, to evade the responsibility of a concern. I did now have a small amount of understanding of how normal people communicated and made decisions, and in my parallel world it had reached the stage where, as in real history say 6000 years ago, civilisation had gained a foothold, but there was little evidence of what we now call modern society. This was at the Rubicon between historic and prehistoric times. Once when my Chinnor bus was particularly late, I imagined a parallel event; a whole tribe of cave people had got imprisoned inside their cave by a rockfall and felt hopelessly trapped and running out of air. By imagining these happenings, it was almost as if I had found a retreat, a place to go, a way of escaping all my worries and dealing with my anxieties.

Despite all my achievements academically to date, and my parents' knowledge of my Autism, there was always the gap, the terrible gap of my missing sister. In 1980 our family discussed the possibility of bringing someone new into the family. We had approached a local adoption agency who in turn spoke to other agencies about our wishes. Now one of these agencies had become aware of a Chinese girl in Hillingdon who was ready for long-term fostering or adoption. This girl was called Po-Ling (which translated means 'Treasure Bell'!) and she was about four years younger than me. She came to live with us for a few months on a fostering basis, but we all got on so well with her that in 1981, when Po-Ling was aged nine, this turned to adoption. She could never bring Tanya back of course, or stop us having fond memories of her, but there was once again laughter in our house. Those age-old forgotten games that I had played with Tanya I could now play again with Po-Ling, bike rides, computer games, sledding in the snow. This was the time to rejoice in new life – I had a new sister to relate to.

My parallel world at this moment had moved forward to about 2000 years ago when (we are told in the Bible about actual events) the world was rejoicing in new life – the birth of Christ. Po-Ling might have been Chinese, but she was not Autistic, and it wasn't long before she found other friends as well. She was much more of an extrovert than I was, and quite confident socially once she had settled into our family. I'm sure that Mum and Dad must have felt happier too now we felt like a full family again. Of course we had the occasional disagreements, such as who had the right on which day of the week to watch the nice big TV in the lounge or the small portable one upstairs, me or my sister. But this was only a natural result of having a sister, and we had countless happy memories together lost in the mists of childhood, and others that will be remembered always.

One factor that had hampered any social development with the other children in the mainstream Chinnor School, apart from my Autism, was the fact that I was up to two years older than the rest of them. I was simply catching up with my lost or disrupted schoolwork from earlier years. But in the autumn of 1980, for the first time I was sent to the nearby Thame Lower School with pupils of my own age, 13. Now most of these pupils had spent three years in this lower school from 11 years old, so I had to fit straightaway into the highest year, but still with the crucial support of the Chinnor unit who drove me into Thame and attended lessons with me. This became more important again for a while because I had 'jumped' two years and the standard of work was higher here, so often I had to rely upon the unit staff members taking notes, in case I had queries later. At this time there were actually two lower schools in Thame, Lower School West and Lower School East, and I attended Lower School East. I was quite shocked about the extra workload, sometimes two or three hours of homework a night.

Many of my Autistic phobias continued at this period, and I developed many new ones. I saw my homework as tasks that had to be done straightaway, full stop. Being able to finish it became an obsession to the point that when I went home I often went without a proper tea, or missed out on a favourite TV show I had been looking forward to all week. Once when there was something on about astronomy for about 20 minutes soon after I got in, I missed it because I was unable to see that I could do anything else until I had finished my work; the thought of having to come back to it was unbearable. I was a bit of a perfectionist and wanted to achieve perfect results all the time, and then became very frustrated when this didn't always happen. I was having to cope with many new ideas; this was the age of discovery and the power of intelligent thinking. My parallel world resembled the real one in the 1700s and 1800s with the planet opening up to new frontiers and new discoveries.

My power of reasoning also increased in this period. I was getting more used to catching buses, and although I still worried terribly when they were late I knew that the drivers worked on a rota of three-week shifts and one particular driver was always late, so every third week I knew what to expect. I tried to force myself not to worry until ten minutes longer than usual had passed. But I was also asking other questions, not all of which could be answered. One thought was: 'Surely the universe must be of infinite size, for if not it would have an edge, and what is outside the edge? If it's just empty space, that in itself could be classed as more universe.' But what I was unable to realise at this stage in my development is that maybe it is just our perception that the universe is infinite. For just as in three dimensions a fly could walk along the same path round a spherical ball (suspended somehow in air) for ever, where the ball itself is of finite size, an identical truth may hold in higher dimensions, where space itself is curved and if you started in a particular three-dimensional point and kept moving in a straight line for long enough you would eventually come back to where you started.

Despite all these intriguing scientific questions, my social life was virtually non-existent, and my knowledge of how to dress up for a school disco was about as far behind ordinary people of this age as is modern society man to a bushbaby. Mostly at this stage I did not even have any interest in meeting people, although as we shall see this did not stay true in the upper school and in later years (see next chapter). But at this point I would much rather retreat into my own world of imaginary happenings, or ponder intriguing questions like the square roots of -1. The concept of imaginary numbers was unheard of to me at this point. I had been making steady if not spectacular progress academically in the last two to three years and had filled in much of my missed earlier schooling as well. But life was about to become a rough ride in the next five years, like a rollercoaster where we have just reached the top and are about to hurtle down. Social and academic pressures, plus fate and circumstance, all had their part to play in shaping the next crucial stage of my life-story.

On 3 May 1981 I was 14 years old but only had two months or so left in lower school. Then it was the summer holidays, which I enjoyed with Po. In the autumn of 1981 I was sent to the upper school. My parents had decided to do this, even though Thame was a good 14 miles away from home, largely because of the continued support from the unit which was not available anywhere locally in High Wycombe at this time. And now I had to cope not only with my disability, but also with the pains of growing up and being a teenager. My strength as a person, my perseverance and my faith were about to be tested.

CHAPTER 3

Teenage Turmoil

Years 14 – 18

L ong, long ago in a school far, far away, kids sat in groups, some anxiously looking over their course notes and discussing their forthcoming exams, while other more carefree pupils were talking about what was on at the cinema, or who was going to the school disco on Saturday night. One person in particular did not seem to be with any of the groups, but always seemed to be walking around on his own. Grasping his heavy schoolbag he looked a real oddity, was picked on and bullied continuously by most of the others, and was carrying a disability that few knew anything about – Autism. This was me of course. The school in question was the Upper School in Thame, and the time was autumn 1981 until June 1985. The intensity of my worries and feelings of isolation increased by what felt like hundreds of times over during these years. This was not due to just one reason, but a combination of several. The chief ones were:

1. The pressures of tests and exams that all pupils have to go through at this age.

2. The fact that my Autism and particular needs were not understood by most of the other pupils in the school, leaving me vulnerable to victimisation.

3.   The distance of my house in High Wycombe from the
     school.

Let us now examine each of these main factors in detail. First, exams
are stressful to any student at the best of times, and even worse for
someone with Autism, where any seemingly little worry can be magni-
fied out of all proportion. I didn't always worry about the things
students would usually worry about. For example, with many of these
exams, especially the morning ones, I would be more concerned about
the possibility of oversleeping or missing the bus simply to arrive there
than actually answering the questions. At this time they were still
giving students the choice of CSE or O-level exams rather than the
universal GCSE that was not brought in until 1988. While I had made
good progress, I had been entered mainly for CSE exams on the basis
of my missed schooling in earlier years and the thought that my
Autism could hinder me from doing too well. I had other ideas though
and set myself a target of a grade one in all five of the main subjects I
was taking for my first public exams in 1983. This could be regarded
as equivalent to five O-levels at this time, a good basic standard of education. I allowed myself only a single grade margin for slip-ups – four
grade ones and one grade two would be just about acceptable,
anything lower was unthinkable. Even this was on the condition I took
more exams the following year to become more qualified. I liked
being hard on myself!

I was under constant mental pressure to perform well, otherwise I
would look even more stupid than I already did to most of the others.
While my stress levels soared, something interesting was happening to
my mind games. Until recently I had only imagined fairly simple
events in my make-believe world and not usually to do with advanced
human activity, simply because I didn't have the social understanding
to consider them. But now for the first time I started simulating more
recent events in the real world, those with complex operations and
multi-plan purposes. Indeed during the turmoil of my CSE exams in
1983 I simulated events in the Second World War, a war that took
great sacrifice, strength and careful strategic planning for this country

to be victorious. To win this conflict would mean me obtaining my target grades in the exams in real life. We can imagine the numerous fighter pilots, fighting to the last against all odds, and every time I got a practice revision question wrong, one more plane was lost to the enemy as a casualty of war in this parallel world.

This imaginary conflict went on for several months between my mock exams and the real ones, and at the beginning the odds were not looking good for a victory. My exam technique was not yet perfected, mainly due to lack of experience in my trials, resulting in many a grade two instead of a grade one – so the enemy 'had the upper hand' in my mind. It was often necessary to work through a problem several times or to look at it from a different angle before really understanding it. Or I could break a seemingly very difficult problem down into a sequence of simpler ones and work through these one by one to achieve the main goal. This was where the multi-plan operation policy sprang to mind in my parallel world. It was through a combination of these revision techniques, and a lot of help from the resource unit's staff and my parents, that all turned out as it did in real history – this country was victorious in the Second World War and I did meet my target, although only just, four ones and a two. But the fact that I had set myself a difficult target and achieved it in what was then the most advanced work I had ever dealt with was a fundamentally crucial success story, not just for that particular moment, but also giving me a firm foundation for more advanced work to come.

In the next two years I took several more exams and did reasonably well, but not brilliantly in my view. I managed a grade A in O-level physics, but was disappointed when I only got a grade B in both O- and A-level Maths, my favourite subject. In the Advanced level I studied pure Maths and statistics, got nearly 100 per cent in two papers and then had a real off day with the third, mainly due to not organising my time well enough. It was still a victory for me in a moral sense, however, since my target grades were A or B, anything less constituting a failure. About the only exam I definitely failed was human biology, which had aspects of, wait for it, socialising in modern culture – thinking back I was not too surprised. I had started calling myself the nearly man, getting four grade one CSEs and one grade two CSE instead of five grade one CSEs, and then getting these B grades instead of As, as if always just missing out on perfection. We shall see in a later chapter that this fact comes into the equation again at a far higher level of work.

Now the second factor – while my academic progress had been a struggle at times, at least it had a successful conclusion. On the other hand my reaction to most of the other pupils in the school was nothing short of disastrous. Youngsters of this age can be cruel and they will pick on anyone who looks or acts different. Groups of bullies called me every name under the sun, although stupid and thick were especially frequent. This went on and on for years until I almost believed them, and felt the laughing-stock of the school. To get an idea of how miserable I felt, let us make another comparison. Suppose a man with a wooden leg is ordered to climb up a 50-rung ladder by himself. It takes him five hours to climb up to the forty-ninth rung, and then a nasty stranger comes and pushes him down to the ground again. Back up the poor man has to clamber, taking another five hours. Now imagine this occurring about five or six times over and this approaches the frustration and hurt that I felt.

In a small handful of cases I was physically hit by the bullies. One particular incident stands out when a big boy started threatening me with a large bargepole – it seemed as if every time I went round a corner he was there. He said he was going to 'get me' and teach me a lesson. This petrified me and I couldn't figure out what I had done to make him do this. It started affecting my health and I was losing sleep. Eventually, after what seemed like for ever but was probably only a couple of months, I managed to identify the boy to a member of staff. It turned out that he was attending the nearby young offenders institution. Even though he largely ignored me after that, to this day I'm usually very nervous of physical violence, especially from strange or large burly men. I found myself retreating once more into my fantasy world to find a way of coping with all the stress; the army in this parallel world had been inventing all sorts of new devices to help me cope in real life. Let's look briefly at two such devices, and the reason behind their use.

The first case would arise whenever a particular bully started teasing me or calling me names. I would try to ignore it and get away from the bully at the time (since I was afraid of physical attack) but when I got round the corner I would fall flat on the ground and pretend to faint. In my parallel world a whole group of bullies had just been struck down with a chemical weapon attack, meaning that they would never be able to tease me again. The second device was the instant grenade, similar in pattern to the above, but accompanied by me making an explosive sound as I fell to the ground. Sometimes I imagined that soldiers of my own were lost in this way in the conflict against the bullies, but then when I got home where I always felt much safer I thought of a general sheltered under armed guard. At home I used to shout out: 'Bullies! You may be able to get the soldiers on the front line, but you'll never get the higher ranks of military personnel in their protective bunkers, and therefore you can't win!'

To summarise then, it helped me to think of events like these, which happened in minor conflicts all over the world, because where of course it was totally fictitious I felt I had a place to retreat to, a place of safety where I could restock things, muster up new strength and bravery and assess the best methods of protection from mental and physical abuse. We all have to find a way to get rid of our frustrations – buying a punchbag might help some! A further reason for falling down on purpose was to look unhappy, as if to say to the bully, 'Well look, I'm so miserable already that if you can hurt me when I'm like this it won't make much difference, will it?' I felt the vast majority of the pupils at school failed to understand my various phobias and dis-ability, many with good reason as I expect few had ever heard of Autism. This is fair enough, but why couldn't many of them just get on with their lives instead of being unkind to me? That's all I would have hoped for.

There were one or two students who did not tease me in my years spent here – I even had a crush on one girl in the year above me. She was rather clever academically and did well in her O-levels, including a top grade in her Maths. She was also of Scorpion star sign and very determined, but it was the fact that she appeared to be friendly and wanted to talk that made a big impression on me. After all, I was not used to people being nice. She came from a big family with about eight sisters but I can only remember one clearly. I believe this sister got a B in her O-level Maths and both sisters were in the same academic year. She then left school in December 1982 to work in a local supermarket where I used to try and make myself go to say hello, but was terribly nervous about it for fear of looking stupid – I felt as if I was walking the tightrope with no safety net! On the other hand I was so pleased at having found someone friendly that I thought it would help me socially if I was able to talk back. I also remember however that at one stage another boy warned me to stay away from this girl.

The third main reason for my increasing feelings of isolation was the sheer distance of my home to the school. I was now commuting not just the ten miles or so to Chinnor but an extra four to Thame. This involved nearly an hour's bus ride every day. On two or three occasions during my time at that school a disco was held, and I got very upset when I was asked to go and had to say no, simply because I lived too far away. Indeed when I told some of the students where I lived, either they had no idea where High Wycombe was or thought I was making the whole thing up. But the harsh truth of the matter is that even if I could have gone I would most probably have been unable to cope socially. As I've mentioned elsewhere, my idea of what to wear on its own was as unknown as modern technology is to a bushbaby. I could not really expect the other students to understand my disability, which was not very well known even among adults, but with every passing day I found myself sinking deeper into the midst of isolation. The actual time on the bus allowed this. Let us examine briefly why.

Taking the journey from Thame back to High Wycombe (the trip from High Wycombe was similar in reverse), there were quite a few other school pupils at the beginning and most of these commuted to Chinnor, perhaps one or two at the top of Chinnor Hill, then usually for the remaining ten miles I was the only passenger. Sometimes the bus drove very quickly along this largely straight region of road with its engine roaring loudly, when my whole body would shake while my heart beat faster. I was making a comparison with the bus engine sounding angry. This anger represented my frustration at feeling utterly alone in this bewildering world, not just with my disability, but also with being the one pupil who had to travel all this way, battling against the odds, like a single ant lost in the middle of the Sahara desert. The fact that the school I attended was the correct one academically is not in question, since I would never have had the vital continued support from the unit locally in High Wycombe, and socially would have been even worse locally, but nothing, absolutely nothing, could take away this intense feeling of being unique, so different from everyone else, and with every day the feelings intensified further.

I can remember many other things about what happened to me socially in my school years – the things people said, many of their names, even the licence plate on one of their cars, will be deep in my memory and will remain there always. When and if I get to 70, when most of these people will have forgotten I even existed, I will still remember every single detail as accurately as if it were yesterday. But the critical fact remains that with all of them, even the girl I had a crush on, I never really knew them as individual people. My disability and the distance from school never allowed me to. Talking on the school bench was about as far as I got to making a friend. I had built things up in my mind out of all proportion, but this was very different from the real thing. Soon it will be time to move on, and we can't dwell on events in the past that we have no control over. It is for this reason, and in the interests of the privacy of individual lives, that I will not be reproducing any more of these memories here, either with the bullies (who hopefully will have mended their ways) or with the kinder people. They all now have their own lives to live. My only wish is that they know (through reading this perhaps!) how I felt.

I have stated already the crucial aspect of support from the trained staff at the Autistic unit throughout my school years. We shall see shortly just how crucial it was when I find myself in a situation without this support. I had only turned 18 about a month earlier when in June 1985 I finally left school with my A-level studies finished. I left behind the comfort of routine and faced the outside world for the first time. My next academic adventure started in September 1985 at the local High Wycombe college to study for what I thought would be a two-year computer course. At this time I was still not certain what type of job I eventually wanted and my family thought it a good idea to try this. After all, this was the time (mid-1980s) when computers were first becoming readily available to the home user, and this also was something of the future (nearly all jobs now and many then used computers in some form or another).

It all started off well enough. I was excited about a new course and pleased to be far away from the Thame bullies that had haunted me for so many years. Who knows, I thought, I may even learn how to socialise now in a place closer to home, and become more confident in that respect. I made a promise to myself on the first couple of days of term to try to talk to and make a real effort to get to know some of the other students. Indeed I did manage a few intelligent conversations. But two crucial facts had been overlooked, facts that were to become the cause of another of those terrible twists of fate which would ensure that I would never have the chance to finish this course. The first of these reasons was that the contents of the course had been misunderstood by all of us in the family. The work did indeed have some computing in it, but was not solely a computer learning process. Instead there were many other modules or elements associated with it. That is to say it was not so much concerned with the machine operation in itself, but the implications in modern society.

I soon started running into difficulties with lots of these additional aspects of the course. One of the modules, for example, was under the heading 'People and Communication'. And this is where the second crucial fact comes in. The staff at the college (which incidentally has now become a university in its own right) were never made aware of my condition and were treating me as any other student. Whereas in previous years I could always fall back on sympathetic help from the unit in times of high anxiety or pressure, now there was none. The staff here just thought I was being awkward, and not picking up the ideas presented perhaps because I wasn't trying hard. With no sign of any real help in sight, things quickly spiralled out of control. Then the teasing started. Just a little name calling at first. I tried to pretend it wasn't happening. Then more and more.

Things had become a nightmare again. I was hiding in the toilets. I was terrified of being hit. I was being called spastic, and all the time getting more and more worried about the work I couldn't grasp. There seemed to be no one to ask for help. I had got into such a panic by this stage that even if they had tried to assist me with the work it would not have sunk in. My parents at first said: 'You have always been a fighter in overcoming difficulties at school, so try to stick this course out too.' But I felt utterly trapped, like a man stuck in one corner of a cage where in the other three corners a million ants are crawling towards him. On the day when one of the lecturers gave us a really difficult assignment, plus telling us that we had to decide within six weeks if we were going to stay the course because expensive fees would have to be paid after that, I wanted out. I knew in my heart that this wasn't for me, and that the only way that I could ever be happy again was to break this vicious circle, and do something else where I would feel safe. This was the first and only time that I have ever quit a course before the finish, and I was only there about one month. But sometimes in life you just have to go on your own gut reaction. To find out how I broke the vicious circle, however, you'll have to read the next chapter!

CHAPTER 4

The Working Life

Years 18–21

It was about the time when all my problems were occurring at Wycombe College that my parallel world had been perfecting a new weapon, never before used, in the fight against the bullies. Things were already reaching breaking point when one morning (on a clear and sunny day) in October 1985 a decision was made. But this time there were no mass air raids or soldier conflicts as in the Second World War. Instead a single, fairly small and innocent-looking plane took off from some hidden base deep in the heart of the USA. Its target was an imaginary production factory used for the manufacture and publication of various academic works, including books on computer courses. After a couple of hours' flight the plane flew over the target and a single bomb was seen to fall, but for one, two and three seconds there seemed to be nothing wrong.

Then on the fourth second after that bomb had dropped came a brilliant flash of light as bright as a second sun, and a blistering wave of heat filled the air. Then came the noise like a 'bat out of hell' from the blastwave travelling outwards in winds of over 200 mph. One minute later, all that remained of the factory, and of just about everything else within two square miles of ground zero, was a pile of ashes. A single surviving bird limped over the radioactive wasteland, desperately trying unsuccessfully to take off with its one remaining wing. The scene of desolation came suddenly, totally, and was absolute, beyond ordinary description. My make-believe world had just exploded its first nuclear bomb. And this computer work was caught in its deadly rays.

I had always used events in my parallel world to evade the worry or responsibility of facing real happenings to me. But what factors had led me to picture a scene of such carnage, imagining a device 2000 times more powerful than any used before? Could it be a culmination of nearly 18 years of bullying and victimisation? Of isolation and mis-understanding of a perplexing social world? Or a feeling of being trapped in a no-win situation? Most probably a combination of these factors, mixed in with the effects of my Autism which can intensify greatly even the smallest worry. Whatever the reasons, in that instant I had decided to stop my computer course, and my feelings were so strong on this matter that I would not have returned to it for hundreds of years into the future if I lived that long. The only way of escaping my trap was sudden, overwhelming, absolute change, like an insect that had spent its whole life trapped inside a balloon which suddenly bursts. I had never experienced such a strong sensation of feeling before.

The question now in my mind was just how much further my thoughts could wander under stress. We shall see in the next chapter where even the imagined occurrence above will look small compared with what is to come. But for the moment let us concentrate on real world happenings to me. In the roller-coaster ride of living with its ups and downs, I had certainly had more than my fair share of downs of late. But for the immediate future my luck was about to change for the better. It just so happened that my mother had a part-time job as a receptionist at a transport firm called Cavewood on the nearby Cressex Business Park. One day shortly after my college disaster she happened to mention me to one of the managers at the company, explaining how both she and my Dad were considerably concerned about what was best for me. Through this conversation I got invited for an interview for a job in the accounts department there. Let us review what the outcome was.

It was on a Thursday in November 1985 that my interview took place. I was a bit apprehensive about it. I thought I might be sent away at once because of my Autism and the fact that my confidence was very low at this point. Nevertheless I managed not to show this. The first thing I got asked was when I had just met the interviewer on the stairway, before we had even got into her office. She asked, 'What's the weather like today?' I gave an intelligent answer, saying something like, 'It's a bit cloudy and cold, but not too bad.' From that moment on I started to relax a bit more. The lady seemed helpful and I found I could talk easier than I thought I would beforehand. I must have done all right because at the end of the interview she said, 'If you like you can start on Monday.' Of course I was thrilled at this instant, for I had found a worthwhile occupation at a time when I had no idea which direction my life was heading in. It was a job I was to hold on to full time for over three years.

My new work had many positive aspects to it. For a start because Mum also worked in the same building she was able to give me a lift in every day (we both started at 9am). During the first few weeks she also gave me a ride home, but after this I walked home (about a 20-minute walk) through the industrial estate, since I worked until 5.30pm, while Mum finished at 1.30pm. This was a good routine each day (which is helpful if you have Autism!) and of course I was having the first taste of earning my own money. My job was based in the accounts department and I had various duties such as adding up and checking numerical totals on sets of invoices that of course involved figure work, which I liked. In addition, I was also getting the chance to relate to and get on with people in a working environment. Other duties included filing invoices, recording information in a record book, and preparing mail.

During the duration of my work at Cavewood, I also developed a new interest. I had not been all that interested in playing sports, but had eagerly been glued to the TV each year watching the Wimbledon tennis championships. Then, one lovely sunny summer evening, after I had been watching I chanced to walk out into the garden and suddenly had the thought, 'What fun it must be to be able to wallop a tennis ball over a net and make a rally, and to have the challenge of competing with someone.' Inspired by this idea, I asked my parents and we obtained some old tennis rackets and started knocking the ball to each other on the grass that very evening. A few weeks after this we went on holiday to Swanage where I had the chance to play on a proper tennis court for the first time. I was so nervous when I first stepped on court that my legs felt like jelly, because I was really keen to create a good impression. But my enthusiasm never dimmed, and after our holiday I started playing with my parents quite regularly several times a week in the local park, where I soon beat my Mum quite easily, although Dad took slightly longer to master.

On the face of it then, at this time, my life was looking pretty good. I had a full-time paid job, had taken up tennis, and had the stability of my parents' home to go back to each evening. Unfortunately, a number of crucial aspects had been overlooked. I might have matured in the sense that I was working, but had I matured as a person? And would I be able to keep my Autistic anxieties at bay? Sadly this proved not to be the case. One such worry involving my work I had had since only the second week there. And others started to form and build up in my mind. The first complication arose because of my work hours. For as well as working the five normal weekdays I was also required to work every second Saturday. However, the exact timing of this Saturday work was more subtle. It was up to the individual. If you started at 9am then you could go home at 12 noon. If you started at 8am then you could finish at 11am. I hated this uncertainty aspect that upset my whole routine in several ways. Let us examine these.

First there was the human reaction of not liking an early rise on Saturday. I had always had a lie-in on this day until now. I had tried to make this the one day weekly without too much anxiety. Just two weeks into my job I was already worrying about this aspect ten times more than anything else. For the average person it would just be an inconvenience, but due to my Autism it started to affect my health and well-being. My immediate superior, who often helped me with my work duties, used to like going to work really early, sometimes before

7am on a Saturday, so that he could then leave early. I did not. My boss kindly let me start work at 9.30am. This was a privilege and let me lie in a bit longer. But not long after, an even greater worry surfaced. Because I wasn't starting work until 9.30am I had to stay until 12.30pm. Most and sometimes all the remaining people working in the accounts office on Saturday liked coming in and leaving much earlier. Often I was the last one to leave the office.

This fact gave me untold misery. The last one to leave the office was supposed to be responsible for switching electrical machines and lights off, and checking doors and windows were secure. But there were hundreds of electrical switches and gadgets in this large office. I was petrified of not knowing which things to switch off and which to leave. My parents had always checked things like this in my home environment. At the time I could not handle this seemingly huge responsibility that had been put on me. What if I left something on and it overheated and destroyed the office? Or what if I turned off a computer that should have been left on and 'lost' thousands of records for the company? I was also worried about receiving an electric shock through touching switches that I didn't understand. I had always had this fear ever since I was a little boy where I used to dream that the whole house was full of cables and if I trod on a single one I would get a shock.

I decided after a few months that I would rather come in early and leave with the other people on Saturdays than face the checking on my own. But I still hated this. I used to worry from the moment I got up on Friday morning about the Saturday work, and used to force myself to get up sometimes as early as 5.30am on Saturday to go to and hence leave work early. I was never able to go out on Friday night, and felt so tired by Saturday lunchtime I didn't feel like doing much else. I was also unable to distinguish between remarks and light humour, so that when a couple of my workmates teased me by saying 'You have to come in to work every Saturday now' I took their remarks literally, and ended up worrying even on the Saturdays I had off in case they had meant it, or there had been a change of dates by my boss.

I was also noticing other things when I walked home from work. On Mondays to Thursdays as I passed through the industrial estate there were always plenty of cars coming out from other companies on their way home. Yet on Fridays at the same time it always seemed as dead as a dodo. From the high windows of my workplace on the top floor one could look out and see the car parks of various other companies. One could also see the main road out of the estate, with the car parks emptying and the vast majority of the estate workers trooping home at 4pm on a Friday. Some left even earlier (Airflow at 1pm). And there I was, stuck in the office until at least 5.30pm. It was difficult not to notice this each week, working right by the window. I used to combine my frustration of not being free (as I longed to be) early on a Friday with my anxiety about the Saturday working. I became obsessive about the fact that Fridays would always be a bad day for me, full of worry. This obsession was to last many years, as we shall see, even after I left Cavewood, where its implications were to become more deep rooted (see next chapter).

A further task which was causing me distress was in the mail preparation. This would involve folding up large sets of invoices, putting them into envelopes, and then sealing and franking them under a machine to make them ready for the post collection each evening. There was a tight deadline to this, as the postman always came at the same time each day and did not like to be kept waiting. The office manager had told me that this job had to be finished on time, no matter what, and I took this very literally, as usual. If only he had said something like: 'Just do your best, get as many letters done as you can, and what's left can go tomorrow.' But no! I built things up and up in my mind. I lost sleep over it. I used to stiffen up and get terrible neck-aches just with the worry. I used to get arm-aches as well when I tried to fold invoices up, sometimes many hundreds of them, in a hurry. On Fridays, there was always even more mail than usual, since once a week we sent out all foreign destination post in addition to the inland deliveries. A further factor was thus produced in making me worry more, and hate Fridays.

It was not only the actual physical tasks at my work which gave cause for concern in this period of my life. I was also starting to have a medical problem with deteriorating eyesight. My vision had started to be very blurry, and this turned out to be serious, for I was required to have a cataract operation on both eyes. These were done separately, several months apart, and each time I was under general anaesthetic and had to stay in hospital for several days. The part of my eyes causing the blurring was removed, but I now had to wear very thick lens glasses all the time, for without these I was virtually blind. One of the operations was not totally successful, meaning I had to go back a third time for corrective laser treatment. I had to call on a lot of my inner strength and my parents' support to get through these operations. After a bit more time I was able to start using contact lenses, which did help me to see more normally, but I still had to go back for regular check-ups to make sure there was no further deterioration.

A key year for our family turned out to be 1988 for a number of reasons. My sister, Po-Ling, had reached the age of 16 and was maturing very quickly, both socially and academically. She had done very well in her exams. The GCSE was in its first year and she had commented on being one of the guinea pigs in that students had found it very difficult to find notes or books to revise from since there were no past exam papers, etc. Nevertheless, Po was one of the best performers of her year, attaining many top grades from her school (a local one in High Wycombe). In sharp contrast, my deepening sense of anxiety and stress at work was starting to attract the attention of my Mum, who realised that things were not looking good. She concluded that I needed some additional help, but with the unit support now gone the question was where to get this aid. In desperation she contacted the local community team for people with learning disabilities. This was to be the start of my social services support in adult life.

During these years, as well as playing tennis I was also playing table tennis since we had a table at home (although sadly I stopped playing later in my life because of worsening eyesight). The first time I ever saw a member of the social services was at my home, where I was introduced to her and straightaway challenged her to a game of table tennis. This made me relax more in that I was doing something I enjoyed rather than just having to face the social aspect of talking. This lady was only seeing me for a short time, but after about two months I was assigned a full-time social worker whom I found very supportive and who stayed working for me for many years. I also started seeing a trained specialist in London, brilliant in her field and understanding of Autism. At least now my family had comfort in the knowledge that some support was present again, as it had been while I was in high school.

It turned out that this support from social services was to become every bit as vital to me as the professional help I had from the Autistic unit. Things might have been difficult at times with my Autism, but over the next few years, for a time at least, they were about to become worse than my nightmares. I have little doubt that I would never have achieved my major academic or independent living successes that I have today if it wasn't for the support of both of these establishments. Back in 1988, after some more anxious incidents at my workplace, including an occasion when I misunderstood a telephone call from Glasgow when someone with an accent tried in vain to tell me his name, I ended up hiding in the archives in tears. My ability to carry on with the job full time was now being debated by my parents, who had also made another observation that I was almost totally dependent on them. Upon reflection I realise they were right. Let us examine why.

At this time my independent skills were virtually non-existent. Mum was cooking and giving me all my food each day (including my sausages and chips). She was doing all my washing and even putting new clothes on my bedroom chair to wear each week, since I had no concept of dress sense and why people dressed differently when they go to work, and when they go to a party, say, or socialise. My job was taking up a lot of my time and draining me of a lot of energy. I never went out meeting people socially unless it was with the family. This and the steady decline of my mental state made my parents decide that steps had to be taken to rectify this situation. I finally left my job at Cavewood at Christmas 1988, and did succeed in relaxing, at least over the holiday, being free from the long hours, the post and the other phobias there. All the same I still feel today it was a fine achievement, given my mental state then, to hold down a full-time job for over three years.

At the beginning of 1989 I had started going to a disability learning centre in High Wycombe to learn more about independence and relating to people, but I did not stay there long. I remember one day when I went in the teacher handed out a piece of paper to the group and said the words 'baby alphabet'. My first thought was: 'What does she mean?' Then it dawned on me. She wanted everyone to write down each letter of that alphabet. Here I was, having achieved numerous top grades in many academic subjects, and having experience of A-level Maths, and the challenge for the day was to write the baby alphabet. Progress, I thought? Not for me. Not here. I literally walked out there and then, never to return, determined to do something better with my life than to write 26 letters on a piece of paper!

My Dad incidentally was still involved in the TV and video production industry after all this time, but was now working from home. He sadly got made redundant from his other job in mid-1986, but managed to set up his own home business. My sister had gone on to start A-level art (her strongest interest). But what of my future? We are about to enter the darkest period of my life-story, and yet also the proudest in that somehow I was able to survive a total nightmare situation and turn my life into a success story – even in such detail as writing these thoughts down in a publication. The next two chapters of my book will be the hardest to write. Yet they could also be the most important because the happenings I experienced have fundamentally shaped my strength of character, and the framework of the rest of my adult life.

I was still playing tennis and being inspired by several players at Wimbledon. Steffi Graf in particular had a determination and skill that left me in awe. She had already tried to win Wimbledon 1987 against the then undisputed all-time champion, Martina Navratilova, but been beaten. When in 1988 she again had to face this opponent in the final, few believed she would avoid being beaten again. But I had watched how she had improved her game over the year and I said to myself,

'This year she will do it.' And that's exactly what happened. In the best tennis match I have ever seen to this day, from a set and 0–2 down she produced an incredible run of inspired tennis to win the championship – almost as if defeat was not an option, and that the seemingly impossible became the possible.

The next two chapters of my life are about a time when some of my worst fears from my fantasy world became terrible reality. Yet I was able to find inspiration from the above and elsewhere to conquer all odds.

CHAPTER 5

Deepening Struggles

Years 21–23

This period of my life started off with the era of traffic surveys. Removed for the moment from the restrictions of the long hours working at Cavewood, I now eagerly raced onto the industrial estate virtually every weekday evening to watch people leaving work, making up for lost time with all those occasions when I wished to be outside and free while at work myself. Fridays were the prime day with the most traffic appearing between 4 and 5pm. Here is a typical rundown of what I would see on a Friday:

3.58pm   About four or five cars would be driving into the estate. Most probably workers' families or friends going to pick up the workers in a couple of minutes. No cars are seen leaving yet.

3.59pm   Two more cars are seen going into the estate. Still none coming out.

4.00pm   (exactly) There are no cars coming in either direction. It seems strangely quiet, like the calm before the storm. However, a series of factory lights are seen to flicker off. Only a few seconds to go until people start leaving.

4.01pm   Three cars are now seen to race out from the estate. The sound of other car engines starting up is heard. The show is about to begin.

4.02pm   There are five more cars coming out now. A motorbike appears from another road, and makes a loud noise on purpose. When it starts getting held up by the other cars, my body gets a tingling sensation all over in anticipation of what is next.

4.03pm   Suddenly cars seem to emerge from almost every direction. Two more motorbikes then a large lorry arrive. Another rough-looking sports car arrives and starts revving angrily behind the lorry.

4.04pm   The lorry driver has started to ask someone directions and the sports car driver is not having it! With a tremendous skid, he races out in front of the lorry, just missing another car which hoots crossly. The sports car driver then hoots back. These two cars end up chasing one another out of the estate with more hooting and skids. With every skid my whole body shakes with excitement.

4.05pm   The large lorry pulls out into the main road. Hundreds of cars are now appearing. What just a few moments ago was a free-flowing road now grinds to a halt right near where I'm standing. The whole estate seems to buzz with the weight of traffic.

4.06pm   More and more cars – it's hard to believe there could be so many. The road up ahead is still blocked, and now cars form a line further down the main exit route. Another skid is heard in the distance.

4.07pm   The whole of the main road is now static with traffic in both directions as far as my eyes can see. The entire estate seems to have become one great car park.

4.08pm   Virtually the same as the previous minute. Still static cars everywhere. Two of these rev their engines, being stuck in the queue. One of the drivers is shouting out loudly to another driver.

4.09pm   Still traffic everywhere. However, the traffic has started to move again very slowly.

4.10pm   The traffic flow has now quickened to half normal pace. One more enormous skid from a car trying to emerge from a side turning. Again my whole body shakes.

4.11pm   The speed of the traffic is quickly returning to normal. Three more cars emerge. One of them gives a long hoot for no apparent reason. Perhaps just for the sake of wild excitement of being free from work for a whole weekend.

4.12pm   Only one last car is seen leaving the estate. Just as quickly as it all began, the traffic has dispersed.

Until 4.15pm there would then be a brief gap in the cars, then another set would appear between 4.16pm and 4.22pm, and another load between 4.31pm and 4.40pm. There would be quite a few cars here, which had left with workers finishing shifts at 4.15pm and 4.30pm respectively, but never as many as at 4pm, and not enough to block up the main road. Nevertheless, there was still the occasional skid, rev or shout from this lot to keep me amused. By 5pm however, the rush hour was virtually over. At 5.02pm and 5.03pm a few lonely looking cars emerged from a couple of roads, seemingly from a skeleton crew, almost ashamed to be showing themselves in leaving so late from work on a Friday. But at 5.31pm when Cavewood finished – nothing

– not a single car could be seen. The only thing visible was a Cavewood lorry coming down the road.

On the other weekdays, from Monday to Thursday I found that the above pattern was repeated, but everything happened one hour later, with the main volume of traffic leaving from 5pm. There were also other although smaller shifts of traffic leaving at 4.45pm and 5.15pm. But there was a deeper significance in my life-story to all this than just observing cars. For one might be wondering what drove me to do this each day, often standing out in the cold and rain for hours at a time. While this was going on, something interesting was happening in my thoughts. With every skid, rev or angry noise from these cars I imagined that it represented a release of my own frustration in life in being Autistic, a loner, and different from other people. Whenever I went home after the rush was over I always felt much calmer, as if most of that frustration was gone.

I also made an association with these peak hours each evening as representing strength in such things as academic achievement (top grades in CSE or O-level exams). Earlier hours when people were still at work represented lower grades, as if to make a mockery of all those bullies in school who had called me stupid or spastic (since I had already achieved many top grades at this level in real life). Friday afternoons then represented Advanced level work (or even higher standard), for just as many of my bullies no doubt did not undertake Advanced level work as I did, so equally many of them would probably have to work late on a Friday and not be able to go home at 4pm. I became obsessed with being free at this time. I felt it belonged to me, and no matter how much I got bullied or teased through the rest of the week this period would be a safe haven where they couldn't get at me, and I could block them out, or rise above them in the mind. Although I did watch the traffic on the other weekdays, it never raised such intense feelings as on the Fridays.

Sometimes, of course, for practical reasons it wasn't always possible to be on the estate every single evening, and on these occasions I started making car noises at home to mimic the rush hour, and always at the same time as on the real estate. This became as much of a habit as watching the cars themselves, and it got to the point where my parents used to go out on a Friday afternoon rather than stay in and listen to me making noises. The fact that I had more time on my hands probably didn't help in this respect, although I was engaging in some part-time Maths coaching, and still playing my tennis and table tennis. My Maths work was involved with assisting a teacher with various pupils of GCSE standard in her class. I did get satisfaction in the knowledge that I was helping others, and at the same time my table tennis had become quite good. I actually played in the league for a while, winning over 80 per cent of my matches in one sporting year, but I felt that my life lacked direction. I had no full-time occupation in this period, and I was being sucked even deeper into my intense rituals and withdrawing into that parallel make-believe world of mine which conjured up the question, where were things heading?

I had mimicked many real world events in my parallel world from giant roaming dinosaurs millions of years ago to the great ice ages of a few thousand years in the past. This in turn had led to primitive cave people, which then gave sway to more advanced cultures. We passed through the age of discovery and exploration in the seventeenth and eighteenth centuries to the Second World War. Then we witnessed the first Hiroshima-type atom bomb. In the real past, many scientists became extremely distressed about the demon of total destruction that they had brought into the world and called for its research to be halted. Their wishes were ignored and a nuclear arms race began. Similarly I too was now imagining modern weapons, ultimately the equivalent of a 'million' college bombs, as I sought a means of protection against possible scenarios too horrible to comprehend by many people.

Let's take a look at one such example of the sort of situation I was considering. Suppose that at some point in the future a nuclear war really happens in the real world. By a fluke you happen to be exploring a deep cave at the time, and so survive but everyone else perishes. When you emerge from your cave all you see are ruins. There are no supermarkets, public transport, postal service or telephones, and little or no food and drink – what there is is probably radioactive, resulting in a slow and painful death. There is no chance of being rescued, or of seeing anyone alive again, ever. Only two or three rats nibbling your arm provide you with any company. This is what I mean by total panic. Panic so great it numbs every feeling in your body. It makes you walk in a daze, thinking that this must be a terrible nightmare that you will soon wake up from. Suppose you now find a very high bridge still standing above solid concrete. Would you decide to climb it, jump off and end things quickly? It might be the best way of proceeding. But how any rational person would react in a situation like this is unclear.

Practically, in real life I asked myself, what could be the worst thing that could happen? The most important thing to me was my family. I was thinking particularly of my mother in 1989 who had to go into hospital for a few days for an operation for cancer. They appeared to have caught it early, and just two weeks later she appeared to be making a speedy recovery. My mother had been the creator of life for me. Her everlasting love had never dimmed. She had brought me up, cared for me, fought for me, and always believed in me and my abilities. It would be unthinkable to imagine a world without her. I once asked her 'What on earth would I do without you?', to which she replied 'Probably die of unhappiness'. But why should I concern myself – for this will never happen while I'm young, will it? Life continued as before for a few months, and my parents' wish to help me become more independent led in 1990 to me attending a special hostel for young people with disabilities.

At first I hated this place. Not only did I have to face living with other people with disabilities for the first time, but the staff were also challenging my ability to face things instead of being shielded from them at home. I had to perform various tasks on a rota basis with the others, such as hoovering, cleaning, washing up, shopping, and other household tasks. I found these in themselves quite difficult because I wasn't used to them, but it was my relation to the other disabled people that really worried me. Sleeping at night was the worst time since I was often kept awake by loud TVs and chatting until the early hours of the morning. At times the others swore at me and I misinterpreted this as a risk of physical violence stemming back to my school days. One night I was so anxious I ran home (about two miles) to my Mum's house at about 1.30 in the morning and burst into tears. And here I was, a grown man of 23. That's what Autism can do under stress.

Then suddenly my Mum was back in hospital again. The cancer had returned, more seriously than before. Throughout the rest of 1990 we saw her gradually get weaker and weaker, and look more and more ill. She had always been so strong, bubbly and full of life. But now she appeared to be losing the fight to survive. My Dad refused to consider the unthinkable and sought out the best doctors in the land to obtain the best possible treatment for her so that she could pull through. But on Boxing Day 1990 when she was again rushed back into hospital after spending Christmas Day with us, I had an over-whelming feeling that the inevitable end would soon come. I had to do something. I knew that her greatest concern for me was my well-being, and for me to be able to cope by myself. Just a few weeks into 1991, I got my chance to fulfil her wishes.

It was in February 1991 that I moved out of the hostel for people with special needs and into my own rented accommodation for the first time. My social worker was considerably anxious about the prospect of me coping on my own, since I had never tried anything like this before. But I had been doing my homework. I may not have liked the hostel when I attended it, but it had a vital role to play. It had sown the seeds of knowledge of those vital independent skills neces-sary for running your own home. In addition, it was the thought of not having to relate to the other people at the hostel and the ability of running this new home as I wanted that really spurred me on and make me look forward to the challenge rather than finding it a daunting prospect. In this respect my experience at the hostel was a good one because it had really toughened me up for the unexpected.

In a deeper sense I was on a mission to survive. As I visualised in my parallel world, a doomed society facing some catastrophe or apocalyp-tic happening in the near future has to do anything reasonably possible to ensure that at least a chosen few survive. My learning how to live largely on my own I mimicked as those chosen few, working day and night in an underground nuclear-proof bunker, preparing for the worst, but still hoping it never happens. I was afraid of death. I am still afraid of death. Not only for my mother, but my Dad, the rest of my family, and myself too. I used to have a dream about an express train travelling through the Siberian wilderness one cold and foggy autumnal morning. The further this train travelled, the more autumn turned to winter along the trackside, the more leaves fell from the trees and the less time of my life I had left. Eventually it would turn to total winter, and everything would turn white. That was the point of death. I used to wake up screaming.

But at least I was living. I was surviving in my own home, with minimal support. I wanted to fulfil my mother's wishes – this was the only thing that mattered at this time. The rest of my family by this stage had already been told. There was not much time left. They dared not tell me. And yet, the few times my Mum had come back home to Dad's house in these first few months of 1991 I did not recognise her as the Mum I had known for 23 years. She looked so ill, weak and feeble. And sometimes, when you have led a young life as difficult as mine, you can be blessed with extra insight. It is possible to know things even when they are not said, by the way people look and act. I knew I had to be ready. But so long as she was still with us, there was hope. Maybe she would pull through. Maybe they would invent a wonder cure there and then.

Life had to go on. We had to think positively, that was the only way to keep going. I carried on with my tennis and table tennis. I carried on helping students with their GCSEs in the Maths class. My sister Po-Ling had gone on to do A-level art and was about to become a graphic designer. My Dad was still working from home, and I still saw him on occasions. My own home was in the Wycombe area about 15 minutes' walk from town, or a short drive to my Dad's home (about two miles). Yet nothing could overcome my feelings of approaching disaster. Then we are approaching my twenty-fourth birthday, on 3 May 1991, but I'm still 23 so far, I argued on the morning of this day. For I was not born until about 5pm.

At about this time my mother had written a note for me on some pieces of paper. It was a very special moment for me, and one that I have often remembered when I have had to summon some of my inner strength, to overcome difficulties in life. The note read something like: 'To my dearest son Marc, you have achieved so much in your short life, you have my inner strength now, and the invisible but powerful mother's love that will watch over you and protect you in life. Keep trying, my darling, be brave, and always try your best, especially with the tennis. Keep this note in a safe place, but if ever you lose it don't worry. Nothing can affect my infinite love for you. Mum.' I really do believe that a lot of the strength of character I have today was through this love, care and understanding that my Mum and the rest of my family had shown me in all the previous years of my existence. The tennis being mentioned was nicely relevant since my parents had only recently given me a tennis trophy for supreme effort and hard work on the tennis court.

By the time we had reached 3 May 1991 I had virtually mastered my independent living. My Mum had survived long enough to see this, but only just. As we shall see in the next chapter, for me and my parallel world of the imagination, the apocalypse was just three weeks away.

CHAPTER 6

The Apocalypse
and New Beginnings

Years 24–26

The date is Friday 17 May 1991. It's about 3pm, and I was happily preparing to go out on one of my traffic surveys, having just arranged a tennis game with a friend for the following day. It was one of those isolated moments where I was living out of mind, forgetting the major troubles and problems of life. Another minute passed, and then my telephone rang. I picked it up, saying hello happily. I heard the word 'Marc!' This was surely my Dad's voice. And yet there was a sense of urgency in that one word that I had never heard him use in quite that way before. I said 'Dad?' and waited in anticipation. There was silence for a few seconds. Then I heard the words that sent a shudder through every bone in my body: 'I'm afraid Mum's dying.' A few minutes later my Dad had driven down to my house with Po-Ling and picked me up. We were driving to the London hospital where my Mum lay critically ill. It all seemed unreal.

We went into the room where Mum was lying, barely conscious. I had never seen anyone look so pale. I can remember her saying, 'I can't go on any more.' In that instant I thought back to the last few months and my newly learnt independence, and stepping nearer to her I replied, 'But I can Mum, I know I can.' To this my Mum said a resounding 'Yes!' and I knew that she knew that her dearest wish about me had come true. After that, despite the family saying a few more words, she seemed to lose consciousness altogether. Hours had passed while we sat there in a daze. When something so enormous is happening one loses all track of time. Eventually, late at night, my Dad ordered a taxi to take me home while he and Po remained by her bedside for most of the night as Mum still clung to life like a thread. Dad had promised to let me know when there was any news. There was nothing else any of us could do but wait. Our feeling of hopelessness was total.

Back at home that night, my parallel world had descended into anarchy. There was looting and rioting and widespread panic everywhere. Scores of overturned cars, broken glass and cries of panic. And a deep concern that these scuffles were the beginning of an imagined World War Three with mass weapons used on a large scale. After what seemed like for ever, morning broke. I knew I had to face the inevitable. I grabbed the phone, dialling my Dad's number. I heard his voice of dread, 'Hello,' I said, 'It's Marc here – I think I know what to expect.' And yet, Dad replied, 'The simple fact is, she's still holding on.' He had been waiting for the hospital to call him with any news. He had not long been home and thought that my call was the hospital. Once more I had to sit down and wait. Once more my mind drifted into my make-believe fantasy world. A radio was playing music. Then the music stopped with the words: 'We interrupt this programme for a statement from the Prime Minister. An enemy attack has been launched against this country. Three incoming missiles have been detected by the early warning system off Yorkshire. Stay in your homes. May God be with us.'

Three minutes had passed. I came back to reality with my telephone ringing again. I picked it up and once more heard Dad's voice on the other end. I said 'Is she dead yet?' and Dad said, 'Yes.' My world of the imagination had reached its darkest hour. And so had my real one. It's the closest I have ever felt to experiencing death. In my mind on this fateful day, 18 May 1991, I imagined a country devastated by several hydrogen bombs with damage over a million times higher than anything before. The world turned dark for two years. Nuclear winter set in. This was my imagination – a place I could always go to in my mind seemingly for protection. But what protection? For all the agony, pain, numbness and disbelief that would be felt by countless millions in this imagined scenery had become terribly real feelings for me in the death of my mother. The experience changed me, and the way I look at things. Even I don't understand fully how. It made me realise how fragile all human life is. It must be treasured, for we are truly in the hands of fate. And we must realise that everything happens for a purpose.

And then, in the midst of all this destruction of my imagined world, right in the middle of the radioactive wasteland, a shining light was seen glowing brightly, a tiny beacon of life. It was the bunker that was set up to survive against the odds. It had remained intact. Civilisation did have a chance after all. From this one humble refuge, society was rebuilt. Artificial intelligence and creativity became abundant. Cities were built, the like of which had never been seen before, all for the common good of humanity. This was the beginning of the modern era. Shops, libraries, cinemas, laboratories and places of research, every modern creation in the real world today, from the tallest sky-scraper to different religious beliefs, were mimicked in my imaginary one. This was a civilisation created for the good of all mankind, one in which no goal was for ever beyond reach. This was a society with the ability to survive, having witnessed the hands of death at close quarters, having been through the worst case scenario of fate, and yet lived to tell the tale.

And at the heart of it all, protected by yards of solid concrete and guarded as thoroughly as Fort Knox, is the Presidential Palace, a vast construction consisting of a collection of large buildings, with 12 chambers, each to work for the common good. I've often dreamt of this place and can always remember my words to my mother on that fateful last day of her life that I could carry on and cope with life. I now had a responsibility to carry out that task. It helped me to make different decisions in real life by pretending I was a leader in this palace and my friends were my advisers. If I made a good decision the country would prosper. If I made a mistake the country would struggle. Protests and strikes would occur – the politics of a modern era. For the first time I was facing up to the responsibility of my actions, although still with the aid of an imagined parallel.

What of the chambers of my construction? They contained all the detailed knowledge, both academically and socially, that I had gained and learnt through my experiences to date in real life from the outside world and my loving parents and family. They are divided into different categories. Here are just a few.

Chamber of Academic Research

It is here that the solutions of complex academic problems are found, and a plan of action is set up to approach far-reaching goals on passing exams on all levels of work, from primary school tasks to postgraduate degree assignments. It also asserts the best way to teach others new academic skills. This will vary with the particular student concerned, the syllabus being followed in their course, and the level of the course. For it is only by effective communication to the learner that justified and worthwhile teaching can become reality.

Chamber of Human Rights

This chamber ensures that we respect the privacy of individual lives. For example, any non-Autistic person may wish to have nothing to do with Autistic people. I may not like this! However, it is that person's right, and I must respect this. It is often necessary to take a gamble, so to speak, on saying 'hello' or making first contact to enable oneself to develop socially. However, the recognition and ability to respect people's boundaries must have a higher priority than our social wishes alone, for only by doing this can our society be organised and civil. One might for instance see a friend once a week, but not more (since they have other commitments). Or if they are particularly busy, or going through a stressful time, give them some space.

Chamber of Security

This department assesses the degree of risk of every possible situation that an individual can find himself in, from a large, vicious looking dog running up to you to a gang of bullies making threats. It is not the general chamber's policy to conjure up unnecessary methods of revenge or of getting back at the bullies – at the highest level one must learn to forgive. Rather, in all but the most extreme cases, methods will be sought to defuse or avert the situation; for example, walk another way where the dog or bullies don't hang around. It is not just the obvious physical risks we can take in life but our mental state needs to be kept stable. For example, if one is threatened with homelessness the stress involved in moving could affect both of the above factors. One must consider the options and make the best decision possible for ensuring one's overall well-being.

Chamber of Time and Organisation

This chamber ensures that a person's life is structured enough for him to be able to plan ahead, set up meetings, organise journeys and travel arrangements, and also to keep accurate records of necessary documents or financial details within easy access. In order to be able to work together as a team, any group of workers or even social friends must have these skills to avoid society disintegrating into a disorganised mess. We also need the ability to be able to make snap decisions such as 'I've just missed the bus, but I can get the train instead and still make my meeting'; or 'My friend is stranded in the country with a broken car. Go and fetch her now, and leave the office work until afterwards since it has a lower priority.'

Chamber of Law and Judgement

Containing the highest courtroom in the land, this chamber is built on the saying 'Don't judge a book by its cover'. It recognises the important fact that a person's character, intelligence and kind-heartedness are more important than appearances alone, and in particular that people with disabilities should not have restrictions based on their ability to do things. Every individual has the power of the human mind, and there are no limits practically to this. The chamber will also assess every situation with friends on a legal aspect, and will not permit activities which are clearly harmful or illegal, such as joining in with a group of people taking drugs just to be 'part of the gang'. This rule will be strictly enforced not only for the individual person's protection, but also for the sake of the others who hopefully need to recognise their wrongdoing, although in the end the latter has to be their decision.

Armed with my new-found inner strength, I had now decided not just to carry out my promise to Mum of coping with living independently, but to exceed it. I set off on a mission, a bold and far-reaching mission with international class goals; a mission in two parts, the latter of which I am still attempting to carry out to this day. And this was a mission undertaken not just for myself, or the rest of the family, but for every other person on the planet who was ever labelled under the name of Autism. The two parts of the goal were as follows:

1. To achieve excellence. To prove to myself and the rest of the world that there are no limitations on what is achievable by Autistic people.

2. To spread the awareness and understanding of Autism across the general population, ultimately on a global scale. To transform the lives of thousands of affected ones, their families and friends, for the better as a result. To help others work for the common good.

Let us now take a look at each of these parts in detail, starting with part one.

There were two main reasons for this part. First, I felt that I needed to prove to myself that I could set myself a really difficult task and be able to complete it successfully. This would, if done correctly, both improve my self-esteem and silence those memories once and for all of those bullies years earlier calling me stupid, since I would have convinced myself that I wasn't.

Many of the requirements of attempting part two of my mission would be very difficult to meet if not carried out in a positive frame of mind. Think and act positively and it will spread; think negatively and others around you can appear to do likewise. The other reason for wanting to achieve excellence was to be noticed and taken seriously by a largely disbelieving world about the abilities of Autistic people. There has to be a certain amount of respect for an individual to make others want to listen to what he or she has to say.

The next thing was to decide how to go about achieving this academic excellence. Clearly, the standard of work achieved had to be extremely high, even for a non-Autistic person. Otherwise it might never get noticed or generate any interest in the first place! And it would have to be in a subject I felt good at. The logical choice was Maths. I had been able to count into the thousands since I was very young, had achieved reasonable grades at O- and A-level, and was now working through more advanced problems. In the long weeks and months while my Mum was ill, I had found one hobby in the evenings to take my mind off things – and it wasn't going out to the local disco! Instead I would open my large S-level Maths book and sit there for hour after hour solving problems. The S stands for special and the work was slightly above A-level. The satisfaction of being able to solve these gave me as much a good feeling afterwards as a normal youngster after a good night at that disco.

Both my Dad and my uncle from the States while he was visiting had noticed me on occasions working away, and had commented on whether I should put all this work to good use by applying for a course at university. My bookwork had helped me bridge the gap between

A-level and first-year undergraduate work, but my condition of disability needed to be taken into account as well. With the vital support
of my social worker and the social services, in 1992 we managed to set
up meetings at the University of Reading and the Brunel University (in
Uxbridge). These two universities were about the only ones within
practical transporting distance from home, where I planned to be
based if accepted. The uncertainty and change of routine involved
with living on campus seemed too daunting to me at this time. After I
had demonstrated some of my Maths skills, I was accepted for a place
at both on merit of my ability, but obviously had to choose just one.

It was Brunel I chose. Sometimes one just gets an instant feeling
about a place. As soon as I saw it I knew there was something special
about it. I just felt it was going to be the stage of a key part of my adult
life. My course was to start just a few months away, in September
1993. Now one of my dreams was about to come true. This was the
ultimate paradox I thought for someone who used to be the laughing-
stock of the school because he was so stupid, as they put it. I now had a
chance to go and study with the best academic minds in the land as
part of attempting to achieve an ambitious mission for the good of all
Autism. Unlike the computer course drama, the university staff were
made aware right from the start about my disability, although apart
from what we told them they would have to find out for themselves
when I was there!

The second part of my overall mission has a much further reaching
ambition, since it could change the lives of countless others as well as
my own, for the better if successful. Part of this could only be done
after I had established myself a little with some academic success, but
other parts could be worked on straightaway; in particular my experiences of Autism were already known since I was living with it. The
first step here was to find a way to get a large number of people to
listen to my experiences. One obvious method was to make public
speeches. My first big chance came in 1992 where I gave a talk for the
National Autistic Society AGM. I divided my speech into three different sections to provide variety for the audience. First, I explained what
it was like to live with Autism, explaining my feelings by way of

examples and comparisons of events in everyday life of an average person. Second, I ran through key events in my own life-story. Finally, I generalised the situation and discussed how other Autistic people and their families can make progress. It was almost like a shortened version of this book! The speech lasted about 40 minutes, but then I took nearly as long again answering questions from the audience.

Making a speech in front of hundreds of people can be nerve racking at the start if you are not used to it. Like the beginning of an exam, you can feel vulnerable, knowing that your ability to cope could come under scrutiny. The more you give talks, however, the more confident you get. Certainly that first time when I stood up next to the microphone in front of these people it hit me: 'Oh no! What am I doing here? I'm not going to get any help now but will have to perform all by myself.' I can remember forcing myself to keep talking fluently, and thinking that this was part of my mission to help others. By the time I had got halfway through my talk I was already starting to feel better. And when I got to answering the questions I felt quite relaxed and thought I'd managed to do quite a good job.

Talking in public is of course not the only way to attract the attention of large numbers of people. There are other even more impacting methods. One of these is to appear on local or even national TV. Another is to have work on Autism published. All of these things were to come true, but they would have to wait until the next major period of my life had already started. We are fast approaching my twenty-sixth birthday, and before I knew it there was only the summer holiday left before my experiences at university were to begin. I started sorting out my financial situation with my social worker and sorting out my grant (yes they still had these then!). I also spent quite a few hours looking at travel arrangements and bus timetables. There was about a 15-minute walk from my house to the bus stop, up to 45 minutes on the bus to Uxbridge, and then another 20-minute walk (or second bus) up to campus, so it was going to be quite a long day.

The final thing to do, then, before the great adventure began was to decide what the target result of my BSc in Maths was going to be. For the first time instead of grades A to E or one to five I was confronted with first, second or third class honours, the second class being divided into upper and lower divisions. Now there are many people who would actually be quite happy with an upper second class honours. But I wanted to be a perfectionist. I had set myself a goal of international standards to achieve academic excellence. There could be only one favourable result, and it wasn't an upper second or anything lower! I did however allow myself a one-level margin for error – should disaster strike (if I was ill for my exams, for instance) and I slipped to a 2:1. I would accept this on condition that I either took another BSc to reach the required first or, better still, take a more advanced degree. Until I had managed one of these, the first part of my mission would not be complete.

So now we are all set. Just a few years previously I was almost convinced I would struggle to do well at O-level Maths after I underperformed in the mock exam. Now what was then only a dream was about to come true. The next two chapters will reveal how this was to unfold.

CHAPTER 7

University Life I

Undergraduate Study

Originally operating as a college of advanced technology, Brunel officially became a university in its own right in 1966, while the Uxbridge campus where I was to attend became fully established in 1971 after its original location in Acton. It can be regarded as a smaller, yet more cosy place of research than some other universities such as Oxford. This had the advantage that once I had settled in, everything I needed for my work such as libraries and computer rooms were close at hand. My course was a direct BSc in Maths which was split down into various modules representing different areas of mathematical study, such as modelling, statistics and numerical analysis, but with a fairly even distribution of workload on each module. This was in contrast to many other BSc degrees being offered such as BSc in Maths and statistics and a BSc in Maths and computing, which had a significant part of their course away from the so-called 'pure' Maths theory which had always been my keenest interest.

The university used the American-style semester system consisting of two longer terms per academic year in contrast to the traditional three shorter terms. The first semester lasts from September until January while the second goes from February until June, and each of these semesters consists of six 'modules' of study. At the end of each semester there is a two-week period of examinations, which for me was by far the most important period of having my work assessed. Most of my modules were marked 100 per cent on the exam at the end, and even those that had a coursework element only represented 20 per cent of the total marks. This was not true of many other degrees that had a higher content of coursework assessment. In addition, many students took an extra year of their BSc to go on a work placement. This was a useful thing to do provided you had a rough idea of the sort of job field you wished to embark on. I had elected not to do this, and embarked on a full-time, three-year course without work placement.

There were basically two reasons why I chose the course without work placement. First, I enjoyed the stable timetable of a rigid structure to my day, which working elsewhere would have broken and brought extra problems such as travelling times increasing and having to relate to strangers in the workplace. I probably would have dwelt on these and my work concentration ability could have suffered. The other reason is that while there are many job applications for graduates who have specialised in, say, computing, there are in fact very few jobs other than teaching that are linked with the pure mathematician. I knew I enjoyed teaching, but I was unsure where my life would lead and what form it might take after I left university. For the time being, all that mattered was that I was there, attempting to realise my dream in a place of academic excellence, and my greatest adventure was just starting. My course then would consist of six semesters on three levels (one level per year, each more challenging) with success required on each level before attempting the next one.

In my first year at university my grades turned out to be like a dream come true as well, even by my high target levels. I ended up winning the year prize jointly with two other pupils for being one of the best three grade achievers, obtaining ten grade As and two grade Bs in my twelve modules of study. Even the two grade Bs only missed As by a couple of per cent. My hours spent at home in my study the year before, working out 'Maths problems' for fun, were really helping me here for I had already done a lot of the background reading that was necessary for many other students. I had to be able to make critical decisions on the management and organisation of a large amount of work of a high standard. For example, I might have had a statistics course assignment to finish, but also a mathematical modelling task with a deadline of submission before the statistics; thus I would concentrate on the modelling first. If I had numerical method notes to revise, I could have a look at these on the bus going home.

We can imagine how in my parallel world all the strength and know-how on time management and academic knowledge from the various chambers of 'head base' were required at a high level of intensity to cope with the demands of my course. We can picture a conflict where we are attempting to work out the right tactics to win, not with Second World War planes any more, but with sophisticated modern jet aircraft, racing across the countryside at more than the speed of sound. Fields, towns, villages, a church and some mountains all race underneath us and are gone in just a few seconds. The 'stupid boy' from school (as the bullies had put it) now felt as far above those tormentors with his grades as comparing the speed of a jet aircraft to a tow-truck. And this was only the first year of a first degree. There would be many more adventures in the next two years, but there are two or three more important happenings in the first year that should on no account be left unmentioned.

The first point to note is that in each semester of my first year there was one module on computing – the general idea was that the rest of the course was going to demand at least a fundamental knowledge on how to operate them, and how to prepare and debug source code (computer programs). Now while the average student would probably expect to try to distribute the workload evenly among the modules, I found I was spending up to 80 per cent of my time on the computer ones, simply because unlike the rest of the Maths I had little previous experience. I used to get hopelessly bogged down on totally trivial things such as if I didn't know how to get a printout of my work, rather than the actual assignment. These were the only two modules of study in my first year where I did not feel well up on knowledge, but I had come to grips with them since all modules in the first year of my course were compulsory.

There was also the fact that I had to log on (connect to the shared network) and log off afterwards from the university computers. I used to worry considerably that I would forget to log off for some reason. It was one of the university's essential rules that on paper should never be broken, since otherwise other people could access your files. I would then conjure up worst-case scenarios such as: 'What if someone did access my files, and sent a command to the print office for hundreds of pages of printout for which the cost would be charged to me, possibly hundreds of pounds which I wouldn't be able to pay?' Once the computer I was working on crashed while the lecturer had gone out of the room. I then sat there for hours in front of the screen, instead of seeking help, because I was so worried about disobeying the crucial rule and leaving the computer logged on. Of course sometimes my old worries about getting an electric shock surfaced, particularly when switching the machine on and off.

As for the exams themselves in my first year, there was really only one main problem and it wasn't with answering any of the questions! After all, my grade results had shown that. No, for me the biggest challenge came at the end of the exam where each time you were given some thread which you had to feed through a hole in your paperwork and tie all your sheets of paper together so that they didn't get lost or separated. And could I do this properly? I could not! I lost sleep over it! I got aches and pains all over my body with the stress of worrying about it. I folded the papers the wrong way and couldn't get the thread through the hole. Then I panicked that perhaps I hadn't done it right, that all my work would get lost and I would get a zero mark in the exam. Once in desperation I asked one of the invigilators if he could help me tie the papers up. He said 'No!', thinking I was just making a fuss. He then remarked, 'If I started to tie exam papers up for every student I would be here all day!' Point taken, but I think he should have realised that I had a disability and wasn't an average student. I also worried that I would forget to write my name on my exam paper.

In time I devised a system which helped me to combat some of these worries and would write down on a separate piece of paper the date and the fact that I had logged out of this computer or I had put my name on this exam paper. While being rather cumbersome, it was effective in reducing my anxiety. I had also started interacting with some of the other students in my classes, making one best friend and two or three other friendly people I talked to. The 'best' friend was also doing a three-year course and most of her modules were also the same as mine. We ended up giving each other support with academic problems as well as emotionally cheering up after exchanging good advice. Of course there were many things I did not do socially – I still wasn't going out to discos or playing table tennis (even though there was a club at university for this). With all my work and travelling in every day there didn't seem to be time, but the point is that even the amount of communication I was engaging in here was a hundred times better than at any other educational establishment I had attended previously.

After the end of my first year at university, my Dad and I went on holiday to Swanage to let off steam and celebrate my great achievements so far, all now in eager anticipation to see if my good performances could continue for the rest of the course. And yet…sometimes in the rises and falls of life the falls can come just as quickly and as unexpectedly as the rises. In the latter two years of my BSc my performance was going to be affected by a cruel twist of fate, one that was totally unexpected. It all started when we returned home from that holiday, with my Dad parking his car on my road and me saying, 'I'll just run up to my house and unlock the door, Dad, then I'll come back and help you with the suitcases.' I had some trouble with the front-door key getting in, almost as if it had been forced. I thought 'That's odd', but then innocently stepped inside. A few seconds later I was running back down the path shouting, 'Dad, come quickly. I think I've been burgled!'

We both stared at my house in shock. The TV and video recorder had gone. There were drawers left open with clothes hanging out of most of them. Bits of paper and rubbish lay everywhere. My house had always been a fairly pleasant one – but it was on the ground floor even though there was an upstairs as well. It was also secluded round the back of the house and fairly easy to break in for a determined burglar. But we had never really thought about the possibility in any great detail. After all, surely this was the sort of occurrence that we would only read about in the papers? But now it had happened to me. Despite this, I just about got over it this time. After all, it's a situation that perhaps many people find themselves in when they return from being away on holiday. Obviously someone must have observed there being no lights on during that period. Now that I was back I'd have the lights on again, so they'd notice that too if they came looking at my house again. And surely when they'd been once they would know the house would be more carefully guarded and so wouldn't bother coming back again, would they?

Now we are in the autumn of 1994, just a few weeks into the start of my second university year. The nights are drawing in for the approaching winter and I was often staying quite late at the university to finish assignments and work tasks before returning home late in the evening. It was when I came home on one of these dark evenings that it happened for a second time. This time my front door was wide open. The TV and video recorder (that had been replaced from last time) had gone once more. And once again there was mess and clothes all about the house. The burglars had struck again. On this occasion I never really got over it. When they came before I had been away on holiday – that was more understandable. But now they had struck while I was living there. What if they came again and I saw or bumped into them? I was also at university now, with assignments and approaching exams to worry about, not on holiday like before. Now began a period of active anxiety as once again my phobias quickly built up.

I started mistrusting nearly everyone I saw, to the point that whenever I saw anyone in the street I would think, 'Is he the culprit?', 'Is he the one responsible for invading my own private living space?' But most of all it was the fear of potential violence or getting hurt by the burglars if they came back while I was in the house that gave me so many sleepless nights. What if they brought guns or knives with them? What if they kidnapped me? In all my experiences to date my home had been the one place of safety, a location of refuge away from the bullies and dangers of the outside world where I could rest and gather new strength for the challenges of life that lay ahead. Now this one safe haven was having its security undermined. Perhaps in my parallel world the enemy had scored a major victory or had gained access to one of those top secret bunkers via a spy and had uncovered many of my own highly classified set of plans for protection on out-witting the bully.

In the few weeks following this incident coming home every day was a nightmare. Each time I thought I would once again see the door forced open, or the window smashed and my possessions gone, or worse maybe see the villains still in there. Twice the burglars struck in nearby houses. I could only then feel for those people as I knew what they had been through. Then in another premonition I saw the culprits returning again. I felt it in my bones. 'All things come in threes,' I thought. No matter how much my friends tried to convince me otherwise, I just knew they would return. My work had suffered and I had performed terribly by my standards, only achieving a 2:1 overall in my third semester, with only 2 As. This was despite the fact that many of my modules were now optional and there were no more modules taken that concentrated only on computing and source code preparation.

This takes us to 1995 where some great and bad things happened. Although the overall plan in my mission in life was to achieve academic excellence first, and then help others by spreading the awareness of Autism later, there was nothing to say that I couldn't mix the two a little, and I had two great chances to do this early in 1995. The first of these was in giving another talk on Autism and what I had done so far. This was at the International Conference in Leeds, the biggest meeting ever held at that time in this country of Autistic specialists and professors from around the world. Several hundred people attended. But soon after this I got an even better chance to spread the awareness of Autism around the country, with an audience not just of hundreds but of thousands or even millions, by appearing on national TV. I did this by being filmed for the BBC1 programme *QED* where I featured with another younger Autistic person. Let us briefly review the filming they did of me.

In order to show a true reflection of my full life-style it was necessary for the camera crew to film me in various locations, and I had to fit this time in with my studies, but it was well worth it for my chance of fame! One such location was at my local tennis court playing tennis with one of my best friends (participating in the sport I loved). Another place they went was the local launderette to show me taking my washing there. At this time I had a washing machine at home but didn't want to use it in case it went wrong or flooded – another Autistic worry that the programme highlighted. A third place where I was filmed was at the local train station – at this time I had just mastered a long-running phobia about train travelling on my own. This stemmed from an incident when I was much younger and was on a train with the family but we could not get the (old-fashioned) pull handle train door open and missed our stop. I had built up an anxiety that if this happened when I was on my own, or I got off at the wrong station anyway or got lost, I would not be able to cope. But the programme showed how I got to grips with the problem out of practicality because I really wanted to – it was up to an hour quicker than travelling by bus all the way to university at Brunel.

Among other highlights, I was filmed at a special coffee shop I had found in Thame where I had started to go and eat my sausages and chips. The shop was unique in several ways; for instance I hate smoking, even the sight of it. I think it's one of the ultimate evil products trapping millions of innocent victims with its deadly addictive chemical effects. The Thame coffee shop is the only place I know which is totally non-smoking and serves the food I really like – and all day long too. I can have my meal at 9am, at lunchtime, or 4.30pm. It's also very user friendly. I shall be reviewing Thame again more thoroughly in Chapter 9. The programme makers also filmed me at Brunel with my supervisor, who was choosing modules with me for the following year. Yet even while the filming was going on, things suddenly took a turn for the worse again, as I returned home after one session with the crew to find the burglars had returned for a third time.

I realised, after suffering the agony of this third intrusion to my private domain, that I was never really going to feel safe here again and decided to move house. With the help of the social services we soon found another rented flat really close to the town centre and just five minutes' walk from the bus station. In addition, this was part of a block of flats with a security entrance system and it was on the top floor, making it more secure. I soon moved and found that this started to help me with nearly every aspect of everyday living. Every little thing such as going to the dentist or having my hair cut was now only five minutes down the road, and this was especially useful given that I can't drive. It also made it easier to get to the university by being so close to the bus station, and it gave me more time to do other things in my spare time. I had joined Wycombe Lawn Tennis Club nearby to improve my tennis and meet new people, for an example.

At the end of my second year at university, the fourth (spring) semester had given me a further five A grades and one C (shock horror – what was a C grade?). My overall marks for the year were lower than the previous 12 months, and I was close on the borderline between a 2:1 and a first. I suspect that all the disturbances and moving house (which is stressful enough for anyone, let alone an Autistic person) had taken their toll. My best friend at university also had a few difficulties academically but managed to achieve a similar overall mark. Then it was the summer holidays again, and before I knew it I was starting the last year of my BSc in Maths. Was this the academic year when I and my university friend were going to realise our dreams of that first? Alas, for me at least, my age-old nemesis of being the 'nearly man' was about to haunt me again. Like playing in a tennis tournament and winning every round until you get to the final, and then losing at the final hurdle.

There were only eight modules of normal study in the final year, compared to the usual twelve previously. The rest of the work had to be done working on a compulsory individual project that all students had to undertake. This was a substantial piece of work done under the supervision of an individual supervisor. I found my project generally harder than the rigid structure of the more conventionally taught modules since it was largely up to me to organise timing and layout of the work, and my Autism had always made this hard for me. Indeed it seemed a pity that my Autistic tendencies distracted me from what was otherwise an interesting investigation. The main topic reviewed was a study of continued fractions (a special type of fraction in which the numerator and denominator are themselves split into fractions) and how these are used to provide rational approximations to irrational numbers such as π and e. It can be proved that every rational number can be expressed as a finite continued fraction.

Continued fractions have a number of other uses such as solving differential equations and deducing results of chaos theory and dynamical systems. For the latter, quite a bit of computer work was involved in my project for a review to be possible, which again tested my coming to terms with my electrical fears. Overall I achieved 62 per cent for the project, while the average mark for all my other modules of the year was about 66 per cent. That meant an overall average of only 64 per cent for the year, but remember I had done rather better the previous year – 71 per cent – which would count towards my final result. Sadly, not well enough! There I was, with an overall course mark just missing out – a few per cent short of the 70 per cent needed for a first class honours. And I was feeling like that runner-up in the tennis tournament. If my goal had been just to put in a 'good' performance then I could have stopped my academic mission here. But the task was not yet done for me.

Graduation day came. I realised I did have a lot to be pleased about. It still seemed like a dream just being dressed in the gown and mortar board. After all a 2:1 wasn't all that bad! Loads of people just wish for any sort of degree, so I didn't want to be too greedy. Looking back, with my ability at the time (good but not total) I think the result was a fair reflection on my skills. My best friend had overtaken me (and nearly everyone else!) and got a first. And she deserves every bit of it! I'm very proud of her. She worked harder in that final year than I had ever known her work before. I also knew two or three other students that tried very hard and I think deserved more but only received 2:2 degrees. I was in the middle. Just one of the things you have to accept?

Not for me it wasn't! The reader should know me better by now. I had set out to achieve academic excellence on an international level. I had not yet achieved this in my mind.

Even as the graduation ceremony occurred I was thinking, 'But one day, I will be champion!' I had begun to realise just how good some people are at university. I was literally humbled by some of them and this had brought me down to earth with a bump in the last three years. I now knew that international standards were so high that, ironically, even if I had got a first class honours it would no longer be enough for my goal. I vowed to learn from my experiences and build on them. I felt that my Autistic phobias, and perhaps a little bit of inexperience of degree-level exams, had resulted in me not performing quite as well as I could have done. For, I thought, a true champion in tennis is one who can pick himself up after a long hard match having narrowly lost, learn from his mistakes, and use the experience gained to become a better player. In a similar vein, if I could now show that my goal was reachable after thinking it wasn't, then it would be that much more satisfying.

I had now set a new goal, one never before considered, or possible. If I achieved it, I would be satisfied for life that any academic target, and any level course, no matter how long it took, would be attainable. I would reach what I had never been able to do before – reach fulfilment that I had taken on and beaten all odds to achieve what I wanted. I would get a postgraduate degree in Maths. I would have an award that would shatter for ever the myth that there are restrictions on what Autistic people can do. And even as the graduation ceremony ended for my BSc, I started to celebrate, not for the award just given, but because I had done well enough in it to have earned access to my postgraduate degree, to start at Brunel in September 1996. I had laid the foundations that had provided the key to me being able to start my final ultimate academic dream, and to realise the first part of my overall mission in life. My university life had so far spanned three years, and yet in reality it was less than half over. The BSc was not the end, but only the start. To continue this epic adventure we must move to Chapter 8.

University Life II

Postgraduate Study

We have reached the elite of education. There are two usual routes to a higher degree. The first way is by a taught course leading to an award such as an MSc (Master of Science degree). The second route, and the way I was to attempt the task, was by a degree by research. This work leads to awards such as a Master's or Doctor of Philosophy degree. Before we embark on this far-reaching goal, let us reflect a moment and consider the various levels of academic work which we have so far encountered in this book. In order to clarify the situation let us make a comparison between various stages of exam success to that of an inspired tennis hopeful who is for ever striving for increased success on the tennis court.

When we are in a primary school education our tennis hopeful is only just picking up his racket and being introduced to the game. Later as we approach school leaving age and exams are coped with for the first time, our player has joined a club and much improved his game. By the time we reach the standard of an A grade at O-level (GCSE nowadays), our player has become a 'top class' club player in their division one. A bit further on, where A-levels are being undertaken, our tennis hopeful would have started playing county and even (for the top A-level grades) some regional tournaments, as his experience and confidence in the game increase. This may be as far as our academic wishes take us, but suppose we were able to proceed further. In the lower results of a first degree (say a BSc) at university, our player is participating in national tournaments. As we approach the higher marks, our tennis hopeful has finally earned the right to play in the qualifying tournament for Wimbledon.

Achieving a first class honours of our first degree would be the winning of this qualifying tournament and earning a right to partici-pate and play at Wimbledon – the ultimate world stage for a tennis player. Perhaps in the context of things I had 'lost' in the final round of qualifying with my high 2:1, but still got into the championships as a lucky loser because one of the other players pulled out. In any case I felt I had now earned that right. And every aspect of a postgraduate research degree, from preliminary background research reading to preparing and organising a thesis, to understanding the oral exam, could if successful be compared with success at various stages through the championships (such as the fourth round and quarter finals). To finally get the award would be like winning the championships. If I could do this I would be totally content with the first part of my twofold mission in life.

It was in September 1996 when I started my course, a Master of Philosophy degree which researched special mathematical symmetric properties in the plane. The work was related to certain fields of Hamiltonian and quantum mechanics. The fact that I was undertaking this research by staying on at Brunel was a great advantage for me in that I was already used to the surroundings and where everything was. In addition, in the first year of my Master's I still saw many of the people who had studied on my BSc course – these were the people who had gone on work placement so were doing their final a year later than me. In many other respects, however, I found working at post-graduate level very different from undergraduate work.

There were basically three parts to completing my degree. First, there were several months of background research and reading, plus working through problems (mainly on paper) at this stage, for which the starting point of the course only demanded the knowledge acquired from the undergraduate course. Ultimately it would require skills and information at a much higher and more intense level. The second part would undoubtedly be the longest; namely to plan out and then type up a fully worded thesis (which turned out to be nearly 150 pages). Last, in order to pass the course I would then have to undertake an oral exam where I would stand up in front of a panel of examiners (specialists in the field of work I had covered) and describe in detail what the thesis was all about. This exam would only take half a day, but it can be the most daunting part of the course. Finally, if any typing errors or unspotted mistakes had been seen in my thesis by the examiners (who had each been given a copy), then even if I had passed the oral I would still have to correct these and submit a final copy of the work to gain the degree officially.

I quite enjoyed the first year of this course, working largely on paper, but after this things got much harder. First, unlike the BSc work there was no rigid timetable or routine, but it was more subtle and it was also very lonely at times. After summer 1997 most of the undergraduates I had known left the university and I was largely working on my own (apart from regular meetings with my supervisor). I missed the other students, not only for social company, but also because we had often helped one another in solving difficult academic problems and assignments. The BSc work had been at a fairly high level but covering a broad range of topics in Maths. However, postgraduate tasks specialise in one tiny area of Maths much more intensely, and if you get stuck it is difficult to ask for help because there are very few other students also specialising in your subject.

As so often in the past when I had been less than totally happy, other Autistic phobias were starting to raise their ugly heads, especially when I started work on the computers to write up my thesis. Now the undergraduate pupils had used the computer centre machines. These were in open-planned rooms where you could just walk in and out. But there were far fewer postgraduates, and these few had a privilege – their own private computer room guarded by a locked door with a 'punch code' security system. In order to gain access it was necessary to press in a secret code (revealed to the students) rather like a pin code for a bank machine. This was a 'privi-lege' that became a bit of a nightmare for me as my Autistic worries took hold. I was petrified of using this room and would regularly wait in a long queue to use the undergraduate computers instead. Some-times my supervisor had to wait with me when he wanted to work with me! Good thing he was understanding.

Several worries had built up about this room. The biggest one was that I would leave the room one day with other students still in there, and lock them inside by mistake. What if they starved, or couldn't get out? What if I was left locked in there and kept screaming for help after the university staff had gone home for the day? Alternatively, what if I left the room but forgot to shut the door (it was a hard and fast rule that you always should), thus letting in all the undergraduates, or even a thief, who would wreck the room and all its equipment? I would feel so responsible I would probably never forgive myself. Not one of these things actually happened. Yet I was so worked up with the 'what if' possibility that even when my supervisor went in there to get printouts of my work I used to stand outside the room and wait for him to bring them out to me. Anything to evade the responsibility of being in there; to avoid the possibility of making a terrible mistake, and feeling guilty about it for ever more.

The Autistic phobia involving people being stuck was not confined to university but had occurred on several occasions in my adult life. At my Dad's house he used to have a shed, in the garden. If we had the family over or my sister, and people in the shed, I used to go and check it two or three times later that day just to make sure no one was still in there, locked inside. Perhaps the cat had run in without us noticing. Yet this anxiety was not so noticeable when I was a child. Maybe because then I did not have to face responsibility in the same way. Or perhaps it was a worry I built up for fear of making a mistake and looking stupid, which had always been a major one. But it was not only the actual university work that was getting hard. In October 1997, fate was to intervene from an external source to make things even harder for me. The landlord of my ideally located flat in High

Wycombe town centre now needed it back (for personal reasons). This meant all the trauma of moving house again.

At first I thought I would be all right as there appeared to be another flat to rent right next door in the same block of flats – moving in would simply be like moving my things into another room. It seemed too good to be true and it was! At the last moment this fell through and the place was no longer available. The only other location I could afford was about a mile from town, beyond the top of Amersham Hill. I had no choice but to move there. I hated the total change to my routine. Probably anyone would, but it was even more acute with me and my Autism, and I still had a fixation with time. Every little thing, such as popping to the hairdresser's or the library, had become half an hour's walk instead of five minutes. Have you ever tried walking up Amersham Hill in the pouring rain with five heavy bags of shopping? It's endless! At least there was a fairly regular bus service and the bus stop was right outside. But since when have buses been dependable?

The process of moving also made it harder to get in to Brunel for my studies. Previously I had only had one main bus route to worry about into Uxbridge. Now I had to time this bus with the ones going down Amersham Hill. Even a two-minute delay in the first bus would mean me missing the Uxbridge bus and waiting another hour. And the same on the way home too. Almost an extra hour just to get into High Wycombe and back home again. There was also another factor involving my health to consider. Either as a result of the stress of this move, or from increased computer use, or more probably a combination of these things, my eyesight became an issue with a deterioration in my ability to wear contact lenses for an extended period. What was happening was that my eyes were not getting enough oxygen at night with the lenses in. I found it very difficult to take them out myself at this stage, but if I wore the lenses for too long the eyes would become red and inflamed.

I started going for more regular check-ups of my eyes with an excellent local specialist. I often had to go for long periods, sometimes weeks at a time, without wearing contact lenses in either eye. This left me very visually impaired – I was almost blind without special glasses with lenses so thick I looked like Godzilla (at least I thought so!). Sometimes they would mist up or I would get drops of rain on them and then would really struggle to see at all. My university work seemed endless. It seemed to be taking even longer to edit my thesis and weed out all the mistakes than actually writing the main thing in the first place. I couldn't see it ending. Life had become very depressing. And the demands of postgraduate work were pushing me to the limit! Yet even at this bleakest moment I knew deep down that I would rather spend the rest of my life trying rather than fail the course. Without that I could not proceed to the second part of my mission and thus could not fulfil my quest in life. Failure was not an option. It never had been at any lower level of academic work. I had never failed completely on a Maths mission and I wasn't about to start now!

From April 1998 things took a turn for the better. I was again asked by my landlord to move house, but this time I was not very sorry as I never really liked the home up Amersham Hill anyway. My next home was going to be the best yet; one of a block of flats close to Wycombe Hospital, this place was only three minutes from town and the bus station. I had all my freedom back again, and even more besides. After over six months of change I appreciated this even more. Now at last I had come within sight of finishing my thesis, of having it in a good enough form to submit to the examiners. I had made some new friends in the university bookshop who were always there to talk to, comfort me and give me helpful advice both academically and socially. I just missed out on finishing my work in time for the gradua-tion ceremony in 1998 (they are only held once a year) because I still had a few more months to go, but later in the year (about November) a date was finally set for my oral exam. In a World Cup competition comparison, this was now sudden death in the knockout phases. There are no separate grades of attainment at this level, just pass or fail.

During the few weeks preceding this exam I undertook numerous 'mock' presentations with my supervisor and was able to clear up many remaining grey areas on exactly what I needed to know here. Consequently, when it actually came to the real thing I was surprised at how easily I was able to keep talking. I talked for about half an hour and used a projector to display various slides. Indeed I was probably more worried about plugging in the machine and how to put the slides the right way up than actually giving my talk! The examiners then asked me a few additional questions and I think I managed to answer them reasonably well. Then they asked me to wait outside for a few moments while they decided what the outcome would be, this being a normal occurrence for research degrees. After about five minutes my supervisor (who attended the exam) emerged along with my back-up supervisor (it is usual to be assigned two although you normally see just one in the main part). I had passed the hardest part of my course!

Returning for an instant to our tennis player comparison, we still had not completed the task fully but things were looking good for a victory after winning the semi-final of Wimbledon defeating the defending champion! In real times I had passed my oral exam and would pass the course overall provided I corrected a few errors that were still present in my thesis (mainly minor mistakes). The corrected thesis was then to be submitted by the deadline in a further few weeks. My back-up supervisor said, 'Well done – are you going out to cele-brate tonight?' I did not feel like celebrating! I had learnt from my BSc about the dangers of rejoicing too soon. I just wanted to get the job finished and was already thinking about correcting those mistakes. In just two weeks my supervisor was saying, 'Just one more meeting for us.' The next two days seemed to take ages, then that meeting had arrived. We had corrected the last of the noticed mistakes. I said, 'Is that really it – am I free?' My supervisors said, 'Yes!'

It was in this instant that my academic dream really did come true! When Steffi Graf won her first Wimbledon title in 1988, the last rally of that match had the tennis ball hovering for a second on top of the net as if fate was deciding – is it meant to be? It was, and a split second later the ball fell into the opponent's half of the court. I will always remember that match as the one that inspired me the most, and right now I was as happy as Steffi was at winning the title. I felt truly satis-fied, and like a champion! There were also tears of relief. I had worked so long and hard for it – six years at university, having to cope with numerous setbacks, the disappointment of my BSc result, the break-ins and moving house, and always my Autistic phobias. This was now Christmas 1998, one of the happiest I had that decade. It then took about another two months to recover from it all and taking it a bit easy for a while to relieve all the stress.

Then it was time for reflection. I had just achieved a qualification that meant more to me than having a grade A in O-level Maths for every second of a long sunny summer afternoon, and felt I could try anything academically. How about a doctorate in Maths from Oxford? That would look rather impressive. On the other hand, I thought, I could spend another six years getting this, and then someone else could come along more qualified with a higher doctorate (rest assured such things exist!). One could go on for ever. What about three or four degrees or two 'Master's' etc.? Maybe that would be the equivalent of winning Wimbledon several times like Pete Sampras instead of just once. But I also had to reckon on the stress, the amount of energy it took out of me, and the fact that my overall mission in life had two parts, the latter being to help others to realise their dreams too. I needed more time to accomplish this.

I can always remember one of the cooks where I had my food at Brunel at lunchtime (sausages and chips, of course!). She was a very kind lady who was concerned about my health while under the stress of my exams. One day towards the end of my Master's, she had said to me, 'You're only young once! Enjoy it now while you can!' It suddenly dawned on me that I could spend virtually my whole life studying. If I did this however I would not have enough time for the second part of my life mission. I also felt I needed to try to socialise a bit more and to travel. I was stale from all the exam stress of the last few years and decided that this was the time to start to concentrate on that second task of spreading the awareness about Autism to others and helping others to work for the common good.

We will soon embark upon my adventures in life up to the present day, a world of helping students (in both Maths as a teacher and Autism), in having work published and performing speeches about my condition in talks all over the country. But before we leave university life, two more things: first, its happiest moment – the final graduation ceremony; second, a pause for reflection on what this period really meant to me. It was in July 1999 that I was once again dressed up in my gown and mortarboard. I invited some friends to attend the celebrations, and this time I felt true contentment that I had reached my academic goal. I thought back to that fateful day of 18 May 1991. Surely Mum would be proud of me now if she could have been here. I could now say that I had completed all my Maths missions undefeated – it was time to move on to something else.

University has given me nearly all the academic confidence I have today. In a way the success of this first part of my mission was just as important as the second. We cannot have one without the other, since a firm positive background of achievement in at least something is necessary to provide a platform to help others to do the same. It may have pushed me to the limit on occasions, and meant many hours in the study instead of going out, but for my own sake it is still the biggest period of achievement to date. On the other hand I had not had much time for other activities such as table tennis or social events at the university – there just weren't enough hours in the day! Sadly, due to the deterioration of my eyes and the fact that I can only see clearly out of one eye at a time (due to swapping my contact lenses over), I now have to be content with outdoor tennis in which I have slightly longer to see the ball approaching. This defect in vision can considerably inhibit my performance at table tennis.

And that was it. When you have got used to a certain way of life for some years, especially when studying which takes up so much of your time, it can be a huge contrast when that is suddenly gone. As well as various new skills, I was learning about teaching others. I was also about to find out that learning to be confident socially was going to be more tricky than any Maths exam, not just because it seemed a million times harder, but because it formed a fundamental obstacle in the nature of my disability. I had already beaten the odds academically, but could I now overcome my disabilities' effects on other aspects of everyday living? Well, it turned out that with some I could, and some of these successes felt every bit as real and as significant as those graduation parties. Yet other aspects have proven too much (at least so far) for me to conquer, with some of these ending in tears. Let us now move forward in time just a couple of months to September 1999. This will be the next key stage of my life-story – and all will be revealed in Chapter 9.

CHAPTER 9

Years 31 to the Present Day

We begin this chapter with another 'high-level' talk I gave about my disability, this time at Christ Church in Oxford. Even if I decided not to do a doctorate there, at least I had the chance to see some of the sights of this prestigious city and at the same time continue with my 'helping others' quest. The conference itself was a massive, three-day event running from 17 to 19 September 1999, under the title 'The Search for Coherence from the Fragments of Autism', and included specialised speakers from as far away as Tokyo and Jerusalem. My own allocated speech period was on the Friday morning soon after the opening of the event, and I was very pleased to hear afterwards how many of the other speakers referred to some of the things that I had said. Performing a large talk in front of hundreds is like acting – you always feel a bit nervous at the start, but once you get into it you feel better. And the more you do them the easier they become.

As well as previous experience helping in giving a speech, I have always found it helps to think back to my postgraduate oral talk in front of those examiners. Considering the many years of work at stake if I had messed up that one, then giving a public Autism talk never seems quite as bad. In most modern events I have been over similar topics so often in the past that a lot of detail is now memorised, and only occasionally do I have to refer to my set of notes. I actually prefer the bigger events, for they have a special feeling about them as if I am participating on the world stage, rather like playing on the centre court at Wimbledon! Mostly the audiences have been very receptive, although in some of the smaller events I've had some odd things happen, like one person falling asleep and another bursting out laughing in the middle of my speech because of this.

Obviously I am not making speeches all the time, and I have started a number of new activities to fill my days. One of the key ones in terms of work was that I started to help some of the people from the Autistic unit next to the Upper School in Thame. I had already done some teaching on various levels both before and during university (where I helped some foundation students in a class to bridge the gap between A-level and first degree work in Maths during my Master's course), and now I wished to do more. One of the first things you will learn about teaching is exactly how much you don't know, or have forgotten, since the students always seem to ask you about these topics! But there's a lot more knowledge than just 'knowing the subject' that was required for me to teach effectively.

Communication, and achieving this effectively, is the vital key. No matter how many degrees or doctorates someone has, if he can't communicate his skills effectively to the learner, he can't be a teacher. Just because I knew the subject didn't mean that they did. Sometimes it feels like trying to tell someone to go and write an essay in French when they know nothing of the language. In a way, teaching the Autistic children in Thame (the Autistic unit here was set up after my schooldays) was rather harder than students without the disability, since communication with them was that bit more difficult. Often it was quite hard just to keep their attention. On the other hand, working here was better than before because I felt in a safe environment with staff who totally understood me. This brings us to another interesting point. I have also had numerous requests from students for help I have been unable to give, simply because I didn't have a safe environment in which to teach them. Let's examine why.

My lack of social experience and confidence, my fear of the unknown and physical harm, plus my overriding anxiety about people taking advantage of me due to my vulnerability, was affecting me to such an extent that I was not able to go to a student's house, for example, in order to help them. My list of worries was endless. What if they had a big dog that attacked me? What if I had to ask them for a lift home because I can't drive and they or their family ended up kidnapping me? What if they hated me in secret and gave me a drugged drink or poisoned food? What if their partner or husband got the wrong idea and thought I wanted more than just helping them with their Maths, and promptly smashed my face in to teach me a lesson? This incredible feeling of mistrust used to be present with nearly everyone outside my immediate family, even with people I knew quite well. And on occasions I still feel like this with people I don't know well.

Finding people hard to trust has also meant lost opportunities, socially as well as workwise. Often when I have met someone who appears nice and friendly, or if I can see they need help, I'm filled with a strong desire to help them and make them happy – after all, what else are friends for? But then I hesitate or pull back from the opportunity because of my apprehension of the unknown, and having to trust someone. This makes me very sad on occasions and makes me wish intensely to be without Autism. It's almost as if I'm looking out of a long dark tunnel at the rest of the world and every time I try to get close to someone near the entrance I'm magically pulled further back into the tunnel. I used to go up to the local graveyard where my Mum was buried, and sometimes cried my heart out up there for hours on end because I felt so isolated.

Another factor that has stopped me making further progress is a fear that I will somehow invade people's privacy without meaning to, or that they will get the wrong idea on my intentions. For instance, the type of socialising I would wish for would be to trust someone enough to go for walks, visit the cinema, play tennis with them, maybe go on a shopping trip in London, but not involve myself with a more romantic and serious relationship, or get married. I am not yet ready for these things, indeed I may never be. One thing seems certain, however.

Unless I am given the chance to master many of the social skills needed to maintain successful 'basics' friendships I will never be able to make progress or break the cycle of my Autistic phobias of finding it hard to trust others. Consequently it is these basic skills that I hope to work on in the foreseeable future.

There have been a few success stories socially to date. While working in Thame I had started going more frequently into the Coffee House restaurant, which I mentioned earlier. Not only was the food top quality, but you were always guaranteed a friendly service. I started feeling very comfortable in there and was able to talk quite fluently to most of the staff. Many of the younger ladies who worked there (especially at the weekends) attended my school in Thame and I had the chance to help some of them with their Maths, as well as telling them some great jokes (well that's a matter of opinion!). These were chances to interact with people that I would never get in High Wycombe's food places. There were also several other shops in Thame that gave friendly service, including a paper shop called the Chocolate Box, and one of the few places to sell fruit polos (I don't like any other kind) as well as delicious chocolate frogs.

Most of the restaurants in High Wycombe are totally unsuitable for me, as few sell sausages and chips, and even those that do have very complicated rules on when you can eat them. In one place, for example, you have to have the sausages before 10.30am, otherwise they've run out and don't sell 'breakfast' things after this time. You can't have chips before 12 noon because that's when they serve the lunches, but you can't have them after 2pm either because then they're selling afternoon snacks. It's so involved. I've often had to go in twice in one day when I couldn't get to Thame just to eat my usual meal. In sharp contrast, the Thame coffee shop serves me my full meal at any time in the day, from 8.30am until just before 5pm. There are other factors too which put me off places in Wycombe. There is the fact that most of the food is not nearly as tasty. Most of the takeaway places put so much salt on their chips they taste horrible, or don't even provide you with a proper fork. And Wycombe is a less friendly or cosy place than Thame. Instead it's more like London. People serve you, and that's it. I hardly ever get a chance to chat.

The biggest factor though, apart from decent hours and no social opportunities for a friendly service, which puts me off eating in Wycombe is the chain smokers, who soon get to work each day, lighting up their precious fags often before they've had anything to eat or drink. Mind you, if other people wish to use a product with several thousand poisonous chemicals in it, then it is their choice because of their freedom of choice of individual lives. However, it's an invasion of my privacy if I have to start breathing the stuff in as well! Consequently I will go to almost any lengths to get to that coffee shop in Thame to savour the thought of a lovely meal in a clean, comfortable, fresh air environment. Not just in the week when I'm working nearby, but at weekends and Sundays as well. Sundays in particular are where the fun really starts, when there is virtually no public transport at all. Let us look at how long a trip to Thame from High Wycombe could take on a Sunday or public holiday.

First, there is no direct bus whatsoever, so first you have to go to either Aylesbury or Oxford and then catch the bus in from there. I don't often catch the first bus into Aylesbury, but suppose I did, I would leave High Wycombe at 9.45am and arrive in Aylesbury about 10.30am. But then I'm stuck in Aylesbury for over an hour until 11.40am when one of the few Sunday or holiday buses runs into Thame. I then would arrive in Thame about 12.10pm. The whole morning has gone, and I haven't even eaten yet! Suppose now I do go and eat my meal – the sausages and chips sure are delicious here. I emerge from the coffee shop at 12.50pm having just missed a bus going back to Aylesbury by about five minutes. The next bus back to Aylesbury is about a quarter to three! It's going to be a long wait! And when I finally get back to Aylesbury at about 3.15pm I'm then stuck again till 3.45pm for the next bus back to High Wycombe. Psssh! On such a day, even if every condition is ideal, every single bus runs exactly on time, and I catch the first morning bus out, I won't get back into High Wycombe again until nearly 4.40pm!

More recently I have discovered a slightly quicker way to get to Thame, but it still takes about five hours. It involves getting the train into Haddenham, but unless I can time this with the bus it's then a long walk (about two and a half miles) into Thame along a busy road with no footpath. There I would often be, walking in the snow or torrential rain, dodging the juggernauts splashing water all over me from the puddles, my umbrella breaking in the gale force winds (I've got through about 15 umbrellas to date!). All this for my beloved sausages and chips! And don't forget I then had to walk back again. These are the sort of conditions that I am willing to go through to meet and socialise with my friends and eat in a nice smoke-free environment. I feel as strongly about this as I did about achieving all those postgraduate targets! Once I set my mind on it, I'm not stopping until I get to that food! The reader might now be wondering can't I just eat something else, or eat at home. Let us examine each of these.

I have usually had very little desire to try other kinds of food, feeling satisfied with the one that I have. After all, in parallel world comparison terms, if your country is prosperous and its population is well fed and content with good food policies, then why change it? You could also argue that I have not had many opportunities to try other things, or be talked into this, because the simple process of going out for a meal with a friend has been virtually non-existent and I've only had myself to decide what to have. I also generally don't like less solid kinds of food as mentioned in Chapter 1. Meanwhile, one factor for me not eating at home is the fear of a house fire from doing something like leaving the cooker on by mistake. This deep-set anxiety of a fire usually surfaces at night, for when I'm asleep I'm not conscious and hence feel that I'm not in control. The biggest reason though for not staying at home is that of isolation and not meeting anyone. I've had enough of that all my life and if I stay in to do cooking and then miss one of the few buses out then I'm not going anywhere.

Regarding the smoking issue, it's the people I care for that hurt me the most to see them smoking, coughing and not feeling well, because I know what damage they are doing to themselves, even if they don't. Like someone who is stuck in quicksand, the more they smoke and struggle thinking they are dependent on the weed, the further they reach the point of no return of being an addict for life. My only advice is to pull themselves out of the sand before they reach that point. When I gave up sleeping pills (after my school exams), I halved the amount I had each time to make it easier for the body to adjust. The feeling of apparent well-being and of stress being relieved by a cigarette is an illusion. To disbelievers I would say this: suppose you had a man who can see all right but only from one eye. A magician appears and gives him a choice. He will give you good sight in both eyes for two years, but after that you will be totally blind (short-term contentment, then the resulting illness associated with a smoker), or he will reduce your sight in your one eye by a half for three months, but from then on your sight will be good in both eyes for the rest of your life (body withdrawal symptoms, then recovery for smoker giving up).

About the only exception to my lack of social success in High Wycombe had been in a local sweet shop which was run by a lady and her sister. These two people were very kind and got to know me quite well. I was able to sit in their shop when it wasn't too busy and have intelligent social conversations. In addition many of their friends also visited the shop which gave me more chance to meet people. I used to sing a special song with the first lady every time I went in, and she was also able to comfort me when I was bullied, like the time when some boys were throwing stones at me. It almost felt I had found another sister who was there to give me extra advice. Po-Ling had now moved to Australia, having found a nice job and companion, but of course this meant that apart from the occasional visit to England I hardly ever see her. The sweet shop had been there for several years, but it was only in 1999 that I had started socialising properly with these friends.

Sadly for me this was only to last for a few months, because by the end of 1999 because of family commitments (in London) my two friends had to close their shop trading in High Wycombe and move to London. Of course, when they left all the other people who had been visiting the shop, many of them on a daily basis, had to stop doing so. Quite a few of these individuals I was just getting to know. Once more the loneliness returned, for at least most of these people would have had other places or friends to go and visit. But for me, apart from my tennis club, this was really the only place where I had felt fairly comfortable and had made progress socially. The shop in Wycombe now stood dark and empty, and I tried not to look in when I walked past – it was too painful remembering all the happy times I had had just a short while in the past.

Then one evening, about three months after my friends had shut up their business, I chanced to walk past their shop again. At that precise moment I got a strong feeling (perhaps one of my premonitions) that something was about to happen. Don't ask me why, but I did, and for some reason this time I did look in the shop. I saw a figure moving, and then another one. Incredibly it was one of my friends from London (and one of her friends) who unknown to me had popped back to High Wycombe for a few days to sort out some things in the shop. They had just been about to go out for the evening, and had I been just a couple of minutes later walking past their shop I never would have seen them. In a few more moments they had let me into the shop. I was chatting away and singing the song just like old times as if they had never left. But only for a few days. Then it was back to London again for my main friend.

After the celebrations at the start of the year 2000 had died down (and my fear of the end of the world prophecy had been proved wrong!), I started wishing more and more to socialise but was not really getting any opportunities. My two shop friends had moved to London. I would never be able to get there on my own, would I? It would involve catching the underground (and changing underground lines), as well as travelling on the mainline train service. I may have mastered travelling by train, but only in the immediate neighbourhood, or to Thame and Uxbridge which I knew well. But hold on, I thought. I was the same Autistic man who just the previous year had said anything is possible if you put your mind to it! Now I had to live up to this remark. In order to be able to become more flexible socially, I had to be able to master travelling in an unfamiliar place on my own, and understand how to read and decipher a map. This became one of my new goals for 2000.

I had decided to accomplish this aim in steps. First, I would attempt to visit fairly local places by bus, but ones I had never yet been to. Then I would go further afield, and finally master the London underground, the ultimate challenge for a vulnerable 'timid of the unknown' Autistic person in a place which is noisy, very crowded and can be bewildering for someone who doesn't know it very well. As a first choice I attempted to visit a Tesco store in Amersham which I had heard had a nice café with sausages and chips. I got on the bus and after I paid my fare I asked the driver if he could let me know when we got there since I had never been there before. 'No!' came the reply. 'I haven't got time! If I told every passenger where they were going when they got there I'd never go anywhere, would I?' 'Good start,' I thought. 'I may go five miles down the road too far and not realise it.' Fortunately, I was able to ask one of the passengers and once I was on the bus back home I thought, 'First step achieved.'

Next stop in my travelling experience was to go to Reading, quite a bit further. This was a bit more daunting, especially as I had one or two experiences there that someone might in any large city. Once while I was walking in the street on a coldish day, a totally unknown woman approached me and gave me my orders without even introducing herself! She said, 'I've only just arrived and I'm quite cold, so please take me into that café across the street and buy me a cup of tea to warm me up and give me as much money as you have to spare.' I promptly told a white lie, that I was in a hurry to catch the train and walked briskly on – yes I was a little devil. I was learning some of the social tricks of the trade for getting out of situations and I now knew what a white lie was and how to use one! On other occasions as often as five or six times on separate days a van would pull up beside me and the occupants would try to talk me into buying a new stereo system in their van. Once again these were total strangers. I just said, 'No thanks.'

Despite some mishaps along the way, I had achieved my objectives in these previously unfamiliar places, and now it was time for the big challenge in London. In order to carry out this seemingly daunting task (as challenging as a normal adult making it across half the Sahara desert relying only on a good map), I first summoned the help of two of my friends from the university bookshop. One of these friends works in London and thus knows the underground system very well. With their aid we traced our way across London after meeting initially at Marylebone and found the shop where my former High Wycombe friend and her sister were now based. They were not there at the time, but at least we had found the shop. I repeated this procedure on a second occasion with just one of the university friends, and then the time came for me to take the plunge and do it on my own.

It was on a bank holiday Monday that I decided to try the big journey. I knew from a previous discussion that my London friend was working in the shop there on that day, and wanted to surprise her as I had promised her that I would one day. Unfortunately, while on the initial train from High Wycombe I started feeling unwell and having second thoughts – could I really do this? It was quite different without the 'safety net' of the help of my other friends. But then I thought, 'Come on, pull yourself together. Just get there and then the challenge is half over.' Despite being convinced I might have been stuck on the underground all day, my heart pounded as I finally reached my destination while dodging the crowds of the Notting Hill Carnival on one of the busiest days of the year. Up the underground stairs and into the shop – there was my friend ready to greet me.

That late afternoon and evening was one of the happiest of my life. I had conquered my fear of travelling to unknown places in a big way, a phobia I had for many years previously. And I was socially like a normal person, seeing some of the sights of London, telling jokes in the park (singing our song again) and going for a bite to eat together. I also was introduced to some of my friend's family in London. Those few hours went so quickly I didn't want them to end! Several more visits to London followed to see my friend, and I really felt that I had opened a doorway to more possibilities in general on meeting people through feeling confident enough to travel in unfamiliar places. After all, the underground is a dead cinch to me now! As usual however this period of intense happiness was not destined to last for ever, for cruel fate was about to intervene in my new-found freedom and confidence.

Things started to become miserable in a big way. First, there was an infestation of ants in the flat. It had started off with just one or two on the lounge floor, which I had put down to a normal occurrence in the summer months. But then five or six, then more and more. They had found their way in through a small hole in the lounge french doors. They started crawling on the tabletops, up the walls, and then one day what seemed like hundreds infested the kitchen. We attempted to treat it by buying some ant poison. The idea was that the ants would walk in this poison and take it back to their nest, eventually killing them. But I simply sat for hours watching them, becoming a prisoner in my own home as my Autistic worries took over once again.

I became paranoid about cleanliness. What if the ants didn't carry the poison home, but crawled into my food in the kitchen and poisoned that instead? What if I trod in the poison or if a visitor to my home did without knowing it, and then touched other things in my flat? And then I noticed some ants in my bedroom. What if I woke up one morning covered in a mass of ants in my bed? My care workers tried some ant powder instead of the other poison, but I was too scared to eat in my kitchen any more for fear of being covered with ants. Each day I would eat my meals crouching down on the floor in the hall, since this was the only room that I felt safe in. The incident has made me quite particular about cleanliness with food and drink. Yet this problem with the ants was about to become dwarfed by a much more serious event.

In July 2000 I suddenly received notice that once again my tenancy agreement was coming to an end and that I had just two months to find another home. My heart sank. I had been enjoying too much of a good thing. All those three-minute walks into town I had been taking for granted. Now once more my routine was under threat. Just the thought of it made me feel ill. I had everything timed during my day, from when to leave for work to the amount of time spent doing my washing. 'Surely not back up Amersham Hill,' I thought. Actually, perhaps infinitely worse. The two months were now up. Unlike all the other occasions, I and my social service support had failed to find me a new home which would be suitable, and such homes for Autistic people are very hard to come by. I had always been living in private rented accommodation until now, meaning the landlord always had the legal right to end my tenancy for his own personal reasons. Now I was in big trouble.

I imagined all sorts of horrible possibilities of what might happen: the threat of being put into any kind of shared accommodation, for example. It was the thoughts of dread in being stuck in a place like this that had given me the strength to live on my own in the first place. Now it could happen, or even worse it could have ended with virtual homelessness and relying on friends to help me out. I could be somewhere miles away from High Wycombe, where there were very few buses and it would take half a day to walk into town. It was the sheer fear of the uncertainty about the whole thing that stretched my resolve to the limit. One thing we had decided was to go into council property and end the private renting. Otherwise I may have to face this threat of being homeless again. But going with council help was a different and treacherous route. I could have ended up almost anywhere.

There was also the option of taking legal action to fight for my rights as being a vulnerable person, but this frightened me. It would all be with an uncertain outcome and if I lost in any case I would have to move very quickly. I had visions of groups of bailiffs coming into my flat and beating me up. My health was quickly deteriorating and so was my mental state. I suffered from periods of depression and excessive panic, the sort I had not seen since my teenage years. After all the work I had done to help others and overcome my phobias, this was how the authorities were repaying me! Had it continued for much longer I might have closed up into my little box of parallel world thinking completely again and never recovered. Fortunately, my future fate was not going to be quite that bad, although by no means ideal either.

In November 2000 I finally did succeed in gaining a council flat so at least I had the security of that. There would be no more immediate threats of homelessness, but there would also be no more three-minute trips into town. My new home is about a mile from High Wycombe, and like its Amersham Hill predecessor, it is near the top of a large hill.

Suddenly my three-minute walk had become ten times longer. My routine had been turned upside down. This is one of the most traumatic experiences that an Autistic person can have in terms of affecting his well-being. This home is not even directly on a bus route, but right in the middle of a gap between two or three different bus services. So either I have to walk to one of the bus stops, or walk down the hill or cut through the fields, with the same choice coming home. Just think how many extra minutes I would have saved living in the previous flat with my journeys to and from town! Let us briefly examine each method of getting about.

Walking to one of the bus stops is all very well in principle if the buses run on time (or even at all!), but in practice this hardly ever happens. What will today's excuse be? Short of drivers? Mechanical failure? Roadworks? Driver was new and went the wrong way? One service is supposed to run every ten minutes – well I'll tell you I once took an hour and thirty-five minutes just to get into the town centre when five buses didn't come at all! Catching the bus home will certainly get rid of the hill, but it's always potluck when you're going to get one. They may suspend them if they see two flakes of snow outside! So this option is only useful if one has all day to spare (or is too tired not to). The local town is based in a valley so walking into town from virtually any direction is not too bad on foot, but as for walking back up – well I invite people to try it up one of the big hills several times! Finally, there are two or three shortcuts, but one of these goes through the fields, and in the fields are the dogs going for walks, but often just as eager to jump up and have a go at my leg! It's always a lottery going through there. Once I nearly fell over shaking like a leaf after a massive dog raced up to me but didn't even touch me. An animal will always sense when you are afraid, which makes the situation worse.

Despite these setbacks, life has to go on. Against all odds I have to continue with my mission of spreading Autistic awareness. Recently I have started a new task, a way that is even better than giving talks, and this is to have some of my work published. Already I have written parts of other publications, and if this writing is in print it is of course my full autobiography. For each of my talks is a single event, with perhaps up to a few hundred people, but a book can be read by millions the world over! If I have succeeded in working for the common good of all Autism through this work I will be a very happy man. (I have also been helping other academic students not necessarily just with Autism awareness.) Perhaps this is a good time for reflection on just how far we have come on our journey with an Autistic mind.

We started with a young boy with numerous phobias and a disability that his parents did not even know about. Mimicking events in an imaginary prehistoric world, this boy had no concept of how to mix with other children or on social development, being labelled mentally retarded and beyond hope. Tragedy upon tragedy occurred to this boy, like the death of his sister in a car crash, everything being as dark and unfriendly as the great ice ages of the past. Yet through the tragedy this boy gets the vital diagnosis of Autism. At last his parents knew what the problems were with their son. This provided the key to seeking the right professional help in a special Autistic unit. Slowly but surely, this individual gained in academic confidence and mental strength. Exams were always like the 'battle' that had to be endured, but he always won in the end.

Time spent working in an adult job brought additional skills to this youngster, who found an incredible amount of hidden strength by relating real-life events to a parallel world, but always with the ability to distinguish between the two. This gave him the survival instinct and the ability to make huge decisions and cope with crises in his actual life. Then the ultimate nightmare raises the intensity of these feelings off the scale with the death of his mother, the giver of his life. This individual is then left with a miracle – hidden strength from his Mum to carry out a quest to the advantage of all Autistic people. Cities of incredible complexity and beauty spring up across the globe of this individual's parallel world. Modern technology, banks, libraries, trading centres, universities and research centres, every part of the knowledge gained of the real world through the eyes of one Autistic boy over the years was now being used to help him in every goal in his actual life, from helping himself to thousands of others.

We see impossible academic dreams become possible for this individual, through his system, and continued support from social services. We travel through six years at university and past two Maths degrees and postgraduate work, as the boy shatters the myth that he was stupid or was ever stupid, and in doing so, also proves that there are no restrictions on what Autistic people can achieve, given the right opportunities and support. We then see the boy realise the beginning of the second part of his quest, spreading awareness of his condition with public talks up to international level all over the country, and appearing on national TV with an audience in the millions. He finally starts to write a book about his incredible breakthrough, wishing for this achievement to be repeated with countless other individuals. We shall study an extract of part of a book from one of the libraries in the leading country of this boy's imaginary world. When he has given talks people have sometimes said, 'You are too normal! You don't look Autistic. How can you do all these things?' Every individual has to have an engine room – a hidden source of strength and power to provide the platform for achievement. This individual I mention is myself, and this parallel world of the imagination is my power source. The extract from this book reads as follows:

> This is a nation designed to work for the common good of Autistic people and mankind in general. It was constructed from the people, for the people, to survive against all odds, having witnessed death at close hand. This nation has a bold and passionate desire to help others live more fulfilling lives. Let no goal be beyond reach, and watch your dearest dreams become reality. Let us allow a person to be judged in his entirety, to be allowed to develop his sense of humour, his strengths and his own character. Most of all let us believe in one another, instead of scratching the surface. Do not judge a book by its cover.
>
> We shall provide research centres to collect and understand the properties of today's world. We shall have teachers, skilled in the art of communications, so that they may provide the key to supplying knowledge to our children and our

children's children on how to make a better world. We shall teach them discipline, so that they will respect others. We shall teach them skills with tools to provide the building blocks for our modern society, and its continued survival. And we shall teach our citizens to have faith that all things happen for a reason. We shall provide entertainment centres, cinemas, amusement parks, playgrounds for children, and social groups where individuals can develop their sense of well-being.

This nation will act as one. Every individual is entitled to the same basic human rights, and will be treated equally. Any disability will not prevent us setting and achieving goals. There are no limitations on what disabled people or any individuals can accomplish provided we believe. We believe in our own ability and that of others. We all have the hidden strength of the human mind, begging to be unlocked. Let us find the key to this lock. Let us open the door to a new world of possibilities to every one of those countless individuals trapped in special homes or mental institutions, and banish for ever the idea of being beyond hope. There is always hope.

We shall spread the awareness of any disability across our nation to every part of the general population, by way of public talks, TV programmes and publications. Never again will our people be without the understanding that has led to incorrect diagnosis. Parents and families will know what help to give their offspring. They will tell their friends, and they in turn will tell theirs. And ultimately the fabric of society itself will be transformed into a more caring one. The lives of millions of people will change for the better. We shall all be connected, working for the common good. We shall have discovered the genesis of life. We shall have fulfilled, in every one of us, life's mission. May God have faith in us all.

So here it is, ladies and gentlemen. We have arrived at my life today. Virtually every major success story I achieve and have achieved in everyday existence I have accomplished by the hidden strengths of the human mind. My parallel world is a construction out of essentially 'nothing' to the most advanced technological society in existence which enables me to plan and work out nearly every decision, priority and goal plan I might have. My way of operating, coping and sussing out life's complications in the best way I know how is due almost entirely to this system.

The time has now come to make a clear distinction between fantasy and reality. I have always been able to do this. This is perhaps what makes me different from many other Autistic people in that I have been able to use this system to turn around the frustrations of life to my advantage. Every person must have some inner form of strength or self-worth in order to make progress. My way of thinking merely aided me in finding a way to channel all my setbacks and frustrations into one place, while I concentrated on my strengths and developing them, for the rest of the time. And my fantasy world details were just that, fantasy. Yet the achievements I have made, the pain and joy in each of those key moments in my life, and my faith as a person are all totally real. We can never achieve perfection, or please everyone, but we can always find strength from somewhere to give things our best shot. We may not always succeed, but let's just say we gave it one hell of a try.

I still have problems sometimes with everyday life, even today. To be confident socially is the most daunting for me – to go out with a friend to the cinema, or out for a meal, to go shopping together, or a walk in the park. Doing things like these, and being able to trust people enough to do them, would mean so much, yet I have only occasionally managed it so far. When I see people that seem kind and helpful, it makes me wish harder than ever to be normal, and for my Autism to vanish. Because of my lack of confidence, I am terribly afraid of upsetting others without realising it or meaning to, by saying or doing the wrong thing. I wish I could read their minds, then I would know what they wished for and I could do the right thing. Socialising is harder than any Maths equation for me. What works for one person doesn't for another. People do not always say what they mean, or stick to what they say.

I recently plucked up enough courage to attend a local disco at my tennis club and had the time of my life showing the others how it's done on the dance floor! I was making up for lost time on all those missed school discos. But I need more opportunities to make further progress. Always my apprehension holds me back. I'm always afraid of invading people's privacy when I'm not wanted, even with quite good friends, to such an extent that if I meet them one day, I may go elsewhere for the next two before returning in case I meet them again, even by accident! For if I did I would feel I had invaded their space, or that they may be fed up with saying hello again so soon. This is not allowed, under my resolutions of operation. And there are always the little things. Did that person see me or not? If I say hello they may be busy and not want to stop. If I don't greet them they may be hurt, thinking that I just ignored them on purpose. If only I could read their minds, and what they wanted me to do. Then I could do the right thing (the prime objective).

The end of our incredible journey will be at the place where it all began. The beginnings of life. I shall now discuss how we can help and everyone of us do our part in bringing some of these goals of mine to physical reality, from the earliest days to an adult in the population. It's all very well having ambitious plans in the mind, but we live in a physical world with physical restrictions imposed on every one of us on what we can realistically accomplish. How on earth can a seemingly helpless Autistic child who is totally dependent on his parents for virtually every aspect of life be transformed into a confident self-supporting adult, working and coping with independent living in the outside world? Let alone set about changing the lives of thousands of others for the better. It can't be accomplished overnight. In order to understand how to make progress, we must first go back to the beginning. We must understand the task in its entirety that lies before us. Discussion of this can be found in Appendix 1.

We are coming to the end of the chapters on my life experiences year by year, but by no means the end of the book. There follow a number of appendices which concentrate on particular interests and hobbies of mine in greater depth than I have been able to cover in the main text. These topics range from astronomy and parts of higher mathematics, to helping the wider population with Autism awareness, to humour and joke telling. It is my belief that different people will have different interests and not everyone will wish to read topics other than their favourites. So by organising them in this way I invite people to take their choice, either to stick with the main Autistic life story or to read about some or all of my interests, or a mixture of both.

What Can We Do to Make Progress?

In this first appendix, I reflect on a number of key factors that were involved in making many of my goals come true, and argue the case for others fulfilling their ambitions. The main ones are as follows:

1. *More publicity for Autism by the specialist societies and local groups.* From experience when attending the Chinnor unit I realise that Autistic clubs and societies may spend considerable time producing booklets about their individual club and how it works, but these are often only read by the people within the group concerned. In order to make real progress, authorities must find ways to release details about Autism and its research on a national scale, so that it becomes readily available to all parts of the community. One way of doing this is by giving public talks and conferences – of course, one of my pastimes. Parent evenings with discussions by the societies is also a useful aid, along with more unusual ideas such as car stickers, Autistic T-shirts and stickers on public transport.

2. *Autism awareness spreads from closed communities to general population.* I am certain that there are many other Autistic people out there who could 'do their bit' to help our cause, such as giving a talk. After all, I have managed to stand up in

front of hundreds and spoken internationally – so come on all you Autistic hopefuls looking for fame and fortune! Get your speech notes ready now, and get down to your local Autistic society, or start nagging your parents and ask them when the next opportunity will be for you to give a speech. Alternatively, you may get the chance to star in a TV programme like my *QED* show, which could attract an audience in the millions. Having written work published (like an autobiography!) can also play its part in spreading awareness to the wider world. The more regularly these occurrences happen the better, for people can quickly forget one-off displays.

3.   *Increased awareness results in more parents recognising Autism in their offspring.* In my teenage years, I was already aware that there was a natural reaction from some people to ignore me or stay away from me, simply because they did not understand Autism and feared the unknown. With improving awareness, as knowledge and research start to grow in each county in more recent years, I have encountered this situation less frequently, and instead, more people seem to be generally sympathetic to my condition. Many parents I have known in later life have been able to recognise the symptoms in their young ones more readily, for as well as the obvious lack of social interaction, there are also many other tell-tale clues to look for. An Autistic child may resort to excessive laughing or giggling, or repeating certain words over and over again parrot fashion, all for no apparent reason. Alternatively, they may be observed to throw or spin certain objects, or lack any apparent eye contact, or pretend to be a robot (like I used to).

4.   *Increased numbers of Autistic children are diagnosed earlier.* Many of the above observations from the Autistic child can occur at inappropriate moments and can be embarrassing to the parents, who should trust their instincts and if they suspect Autism should seek out a proper diagnosis for their child. If it has not been suggested already, the best starting point is for parents to ask their GP for a referral to a diagnostic team for

their child specifically trained in the condition. This training is crucial, because personnel who do not have this background knowledge can inadvertently make matters much worse. You will have read how distressed my Mum was when I was classified as mentally retarded (I would like to set that same person a postgraduate Maths problem and see the look on his face!), so make sure you mention this requirement to your GP. If for some reason a suitable referral is not made, parents should contact the Autistic Society Helpline to ask for advice. (Autistic Society Helpline: +44 (0)870 600 85 85)

5.   *More children sent to specialist units to obtain right sort of help.* Once your child has been formally diagnosed, it can be a huge relief to many parents who have actually won 'half the battle' so to speak in at least knowing what the problem is that needs to be solved. A diagnosis is possible as early as two years old, and certainly an earlier diagnosis is better since more help can be given to soften the transition to the outside world in gentle steps. I have often been approached by parents who have had a knowledge that their youngsters have Autism, but face the problem of having no appropriate help in their immediate neighbourhood. It may be dangerously tempting to compromise and send them to a normal school close by, rather than a specialist unit out of county, especially as the latter may not have any financial support obviously available. Such temptations must be resisted at all costs, and priorities must be put in the right order.

6.   *Demand grows for more specialist help. More units are set up across country.* Success stories in a number of counties can quickly bring demand for others elsewhere. It is important to realise that we not only require obvious resources such as buildings and equipment, but also back-up support from local authorities in the form of financial input. These days we have modern aids to help us such as the Internet, where information can be relayed from place to place almost instantaneously. Thus, any major breakthroughs in one particular Autistic unit or research establishment can very quickly become known

nationwide. When I was 13, the Chinnor resource unit was almost unique in this country, but now there are quite a number of such places available. The situation is much better than it was then, but there is still a long way to go yet for universal recognition.

7.   *Correct support in school life.* The importance of the right sort of help for the Autistic child can never be overestimated. To make a comparison, picture a large jug full of holes in the bottom. Seeking help from unskilled workers could be seen as filling this jug with water – for a while the supply is there, but before long the water is lost because the root cause of the problem has not been solved. In contrast, a thoroughly trained teacher could be seen as sealing up the holes of the jug first, and then filling it with water – problem solved. This is why parents must make any reasonable sacrifice (including moving house if necessary!) to enable their youngsters to attend properly trained centres which can make all the difference to their lives. Take it from me, if I had not attended the Chinnor unit I would certainly not be having this discussion in my autobiography.

8.   *Correct support from adult services.* Obviously, it is just as important to receive continued help in adult life when an Autistic person leaves mainstream education. I certainly noticed the difference straightaway after my comfort of the help in the Chinnor unit. It was as if I was suddenly plunged into the abyss when I left there and went to Bucks College, where most of the staff were not even aware of my condition or special needs. The help I obtained from social services and the community team was every bit as crucial to me as the early Autistic unit help, from giving me emotional support when my Mum was ill, to financial help and independent living skills. In addition, the social services helped me set up and start my university work, which has been the foundation of most of my academic success and confidence.

It is also worth remarking that there are plenty of Autistic people out there who have the ability to undertake university level work just as I did, if only they are given the chance. In my view, people should overcome their shyness and make the staff aware of their condition. You will not be held in lesser esteem and often it can mean sympathetic help emotionally as well as academically if problems do come up. In some ways, undertaking teaching of other pupils is the ultimate paradox in that it demands both social skills and the art of communication as well as academic know-how. If I can do it, then so can others. News items on major success stories can be quick to spread, and will help quicken the process of awareness across the country. This procedure, leading to further research and units being set up, which in turn leads to more successful people with Autism spreading awareness, must be continued many times over. This could take some time, but it is vital if there is to be an eventual national or even international understanding of the condition.

9. *Help and assistance at a job.* More generally, it will often be the things most of us take for granted, such as 'rest periods' in the workplace, that will prove more challenging for the Autistic adult than the actual work itself. For instance, breaktimes are often opportunities for work colleagues to socialise and talk, or to order a round of coffee, each taking his turn to get the drinks. This is exactly the sort of grey area that the affected individual is likely to struggle with. He may miss his turn to make the drinks, not on purpose but because it has not been written or specified in the work tasks. This may then be misread by the others as being antisocial, so it is important to be aware of these things, and form strategies for coping with them. Even when I was playing table tennis matches, I used to avoid the home ones on purpose for I knew with these I would be responsible for making the tea and was worried about every aspect of this, from failing to turn off the kettle and causing a fire, to not having clean hands and being responsible for giving people food or drink that was not clean.

Other problems can occur if instructions in a workplace are not given precisely or are phrased too generally. Many Autistic people will not be able to tell the difference, or to suss out remarks that require detailed social knowledge. So the most important thing is to set out instructions clearly and concisely. Writing down a list of tasks and the order of their operation or importance is often a good idea, since the individual concerned will be able to refer to this even when everyone else is busy. It is also a good idea to write down any worries about the same things that keep repeating themselves. When I worked at Cavewood doing the mail each day, certain groups of invoices had to go in to separate envelopes, and it would have been very impractical to keep asking my partners every time which went in which. So I either memorised it or made out a list on paper to refer to.

10. *Spreading awareness and teaching others.* A final thrilling pause for thought! We have seen the influence that can be had through me giving public talks at international level and appearing on national TV, and also through my academic work. If only one in a thousand Autistic individuals was able to achieve what I have done, it still seems there could be many thousands across the world that are able to do just that. Just imagine how much influence several thousand Autistic people appearing on national TV or in the papers would have. If this happened regularly, this would be enough for someone to have a mention every day for years. The information and knowledge gained would be incredible. People from all corners of the globe, many of whom would be hearing about Autism for the first time, would immediately have the knowledge. They will pass that knowledge on, and so on, across the populations from the Arctic to the Sahara desert (and nearly everywhere in between) to the Southern Oceans. Our need for understanding will have been found. The whole planet will literally buzz with eager anticipation as to what we can achieve next on the Autistic discovery road. There will be hope, faith and real practical progress. In this sense, we would have transformed the globe with the genesis of new life and opportunity.

To achieve all of these aims will of course take time, even many years. But the age of transformation starts now. From this day forward, the expansion of awareness and understanding of Autism is under way. We all have a responsibility to ensure that each individual is able to fulfil his potential and live as full a life as is practically possible. So think positive, act now, citizens of the world, and a thousand others will do the same. Never again will there be the unknown fear of something we do not understand, or know how to deal with. The journey I have made will be joined by countless other stories of success. And in their joy of new-found lives I will at last feel content. My mission in both its parts will be fulfilled.

The Art of Joke Telling

After much serious discussion in the main chapters it is time for some light relief with a mention of one of my hobbies in recent years – that of joke telling! The interest had grown gradually with an ever-increasing collection of joke books, and in some ways represented a bit of a paradox. On the one hand, here I am, an Autistic man finding it hard to understand many aspects of social interaction, while on the other hand I enjoy and in many cases understand the certain 'play on words' aspect involved with jokes. I had also found something to say to other people instead of standing there like a zombie not knowing what to say because of my lack of social confidence. Unfortunately, as I have recently found, there is a lot more to socialising than telling jokes. While some people seem to love them, others can tolerate just one or two, while others can't stand any of them. That's why I have put this discussion here, in the appendices, where people can choose whether to read them or not.

There are a great many jokes on different topics that I have studied. They range from those that amuse me because they are simply so impossible to actually be true, to jokes about Maths or space, to jokes that simply use a play on words, and relate familiar ones with similar sounding but false words. I will attempt to give examples of all these, and more, shortly. Most of the jokes are only one or two lines long, although I may understand a few longer bits of humour. There are many types, such as 'pub' jokes, which would mean very little to me, since I am not equipped with the suitable social knowledge of so-called 'pub language'. So normally I only study jokes about topics which I know and can relate to. Countless numbers of these jokes have been memorised ready for instant recall, after I have told them many times to others beforehand.

I normally tell other people jokes as a way of showing them I want to be friends, or that I appreciate them talking and being friendly to me, and of course hopefully to make them happy by bursting out laughing! But sometimes it can be because I don't feel I have anything else to discuss of interest to them, for not many others are interested in solving a complex cubic equation or in talking about how big the known universe is. And I can't exactly talk about my marriage, can I? Very recently, I have found one or two better topics of conversation, such as the weather. Either complain that it's too hot and sunny, or too cold and rainy, or boring and just cloudy, and you'll very often start a conversation. I've even told a few people that seemed kind and understanding about the fact that I'm Autistic, and in most cases they seemed very interested about it.

I have only included those jokes that the majority of the population can enjoy in general. The word 'general' is important here because there are certain situations where a joke may not be appropriate to a particular individual. For instance, if I knew one of my friends had another friend or one of her family critically ill in a hospital, then I would not proceed to tell her any jokes about patients and doctors on the wards of hospital, since this may then make her sad thinking about her loved one. In this respect I wish people to know that these jokes aim to make people happy and keep them amused, and are not included with any other intention. I will start my list of topics with an obvious one (with a helpful suggestion from a friend!) – jokes on the subject of Autism. After all, that is the main topic of this book and most of these (although not all) come under the category of jokes which transform a known word into a similar sounding one that doesn't actually exist. Additionally, most of the following jokes are ones that I invented myself, so ladies and gentlemen, sit down on the sofa, get yourself comfortable, and enjoy!

Jokes on Autism

These are jokes that rely heavily on a 'play on words'.

1. What do you call an Autistic man who likes to spend all his free time in a canoe?

   Oar-tistic.

2. What do you call an Autistic man who has a fixation with time?

   Au-*tick*-stic.

3. This joke is actually in two parts – the latter part depends on the first.

   (a) Why did the parrot cross the road?

   Because the chicken was on holiday.

   (b) Why did the Autistic man cross the road?

   Because he was copying everything 'parrot fashion'.

   We note here that while understanding part (a) requires only the knowledge of the chicken crossing the road joke, with most people knowing this, part (b) is much more subtle, and would be understood mainly by those with enough knowledge of Autism to realise that copying things like a parrot, such as certain phrases, is quite a normal symptom of many Autistic people.

4. What condition does a clever Autistic person who likes fast food have?

   Asburger Syndrome.

5. What do you call an Autistic person with a roll of Sellotape in his hands?

   Auti-*stick*.

6. What did the Autistic man say to his mate when it started raining?

    Here comes the *rain-man*.

7. What do you call an Autistic cat?

    Purr-tistic.

8. What do you call an Autistic lion?

    Roar-tistic.

Jokes that are hard to believe

The idea behind many of these jokes is that they are supposed to be funny because they are so impossible in real life. Other ones just take you completely by surprise. They fall into the category I would use to show I am being friendly, or to start a conversation.

1. Can an elephant jump higher than the Empire State Building?

    Yes, of course. The Empire State Building can't jump, remember.

2. When would elephants paint the underneath of their feet green?

    When they want to hide upside-down in a glass of apple juice!

3. Have you ever seen an elephant in a glass of apple juice? No? Well, this demonstrates how good the disguise is!

4. Have you heard the joke about the whip?

    It beats me any day!

5. What is blue and yellow, has long pink horns, can run at 750 mph, loves crisps and sings tunes to the elephants at six in the morning in mid-winter?

    Nothing!

6.   Doctor! Doctor! I feel I have a multi-personality and that I'm 10,000 people all co-existing at once. Help!

Stop crowding me will you! I'll see you later.

There now follows a selection of Maths and astronomy jokes. I would use these with the more academic in mind, who have some knowledge of the topics.

Maths jokes

1.   What did the *median* say to the *mode* after they argued?

Don't be so *mean*. You always impose your extreme views on me the *most frequently*, whereas I just try to take a *middle* opinion on things.

2.   What did the *variance* say to the *standard deviation*?

Don't let this *spread*, but you've become rather *rooted* on me!

3.   What did the large angle say to the small angle?

Don't be *acute* and answer back. Now do your warm-up exercise like I showed you with a *reflex* action.

4.   What did the *sine* say to the *cosine* that wasn't making sense?

I think you're going off on a *tangent*.

5.   What did the logarithm say to the base?

We seem to have generated a certain *power* between us.

6.   What did -1 say to its square roots after they were staring at it?

Well don't just look at me *square in the eye (i)*. Just get *real*! And stop *imagining* how *negative* I can be.

7.   What do you get if you throw two angry vectors into a mixer machine?

A cross-product.

8. What do you call two vectors on a mountaineering expedition?

   A scaler-product.

9. What did the decimal say to the fraction?

   What is your *point*? You do not make sense, in whole or in *part*.

Space jokes

1. What did the planet say to the star?

   I feel like my whole life revolves around you!

2. What did the planet-eating monster say before devouring the red planet?

   A Mars a day helps you work, rest and play.

3. What did Saturn say to Jupiter?

   Well *spotted*. Now you've seen me I'll give you a *ring* sometime.

4. What did Mercury say to its admirer, the sun?

   Boy, you're *hot*! And you *shine* out of any crowd.

5. An easy one! What constellation can also be found at fairgrounds?

   The big dipper.

6. Why did the hungry star cross intergalactic space?

   To get to another Galaxy.

7. Doctor! Doctor! Help! I feel like I'm a total eclipse of the sun.

   Well, you've left me in the dark as to how to help you.

8. What type of television do spacemen like to watch?

    Sky and satellite.

9. What programme do astronauts enjoy while waiting for blast-off?

    Countdown.

10. What did the first alien say to the second after their spaceship not only crashed onto the earth, but buried itself close to the earth's centre?

    We're getting to the core of things here.

11. Why do aliens need sunglasses while travelling at high speed?

    To cover the 'light' years.

Miscellaneous jokes

The next collection of jokes are the type I would use for the younger generation, e.g. children, and the otherwise perhaps less academic in the specialised topics seen before.

1. Which of these is heavier, a ton of bricks or a ton of feathers?

    They both weigh the same!

2. Two crisps discovered on their travels the eighth wonder of the world, a golden path several miles long in a secret location. They became known as the Golden Wonder crisps.

3. Did you hear about the man that took a pair of roller skates with a hundred wheels on each to a competition?

    He had a wheelee good time.

4. How do you carry an elephant on your bike?

    You put him in the shopping basket of course! But take out the shopping bag first.

5. Did you hear about the idiot who was trying to learn to trampoline? It wasn't quite the summertime outdoors, so he tried a springasault.

6. What did the first yo-yo say to the second yo-yo?

   Funny how the ups and downs of life happen, isn't it?

7. What did the 10 pence piece say to the £5 note?

   I'm going to make a note of you. It makes a *change* for me to know someone else.

8. What did the 50 pence piece say to itself?

   If I meet another of my kind, my heart and theirs will *pound* with joy.

9. Why do elephants paint themselves red?

   So they can catch a ride by hanging onto the side of double-decker buses and not be detected.

10. What's bright yellow, has a beak and two wings and is found a mile beneath the ocean's surface?

    A canary in a submarine.

11. What did the river say to the ocean?

    I can't seem to stop running into you.

12. Why do insects hate the game of snooker?

    Because of the spider.

13. An aeroplane has only three seats for passengers but a fourth is allowed to stand inside while the craft is in motion. If any more passengers are present *inside*, the aeroplane will spin out of control. People balancing on the wings are not allowed. How could we ensure that five people would remain safe in or on the aircraft?

    Don't fly the aircraft!

14. What is always found at the centre of holes?

The letter L.

15. What did the first insect say to the second insect?

How time *flies*. Let us *flea* away from here before we hear another *tick*.

Finally, I shall end with a section of creating something from nothing. While it may seem nonsense, such things caused much amusement to me when I was much younger, and no doubt many other Autistic people. You can be assured though that after this we shall return to a serious discussion about one of my interests that lives to this day – astronomy. Before we leave, though, I remark that some joke telling can give a person a character and a sense of humour to cheer others up. But in order to tell them successfully they must be used in moderation, and at the right time. This judgement is a skill that has to be learnt, just like many other things in life. Upon reflection, it's very difficult now to see how the following amused me. But it's the repetitive nature of the paragraph that seems to be common in causing a large number of individuals with my condition to explode with laughter. This could be of interest in research on Autistic behavioural patterns, which is why I include it here. Many years ago I sat down for ages writing out a totally meaningless passage which started as follows:

> I have nothing to write about. Although, as I am saying that I have nothing to write about, I am at least writing something, namely the fact that I have nothing to write about. In addition, while I am saying that as I am writing that I don't have anything to write about, I am at least writing something, I am actually writing still more. Moreover, while I am explaining that in addition while I am saying that as I am writing that I don't have anything to write about, I am at least writing something, I am actually writing still more, I am actually writing even more in the process. And further still, while I am saying that moreover, while I am explaining…

I think you would have spotted the pattern of things – each 'cycle', if that's what you call it in the above paragraph, depends on the previous one, and is longer that its predecessor; a certain mathematical breakdown, almost like a progression of sets, each one a subset of the next. Could this have been me subconsciously creating mathematical ideas and patterns in my mind, even though the English 'sense' was just nonsense? Or could it be a sense of incredible mumbo-jumbo in the paragraph that amused me, in comparison with what the social adult world must seem to an Autistic youngster? In any case, this is now in the past. It is time for more adult discussion on the universe, and I will not be dwelling on the origin or causes of unusual types of Autistic amusement any further, but will leave this to the reader to make up their own views.

The Universe

M y interest in astronomy stems from when I was a little boy. I used to have a telescope and loved visiting the Planetarium in London. I also had a vast collection of space books which I would read repeatedly for many hours. There may even be a deeper sense to this hobby. Being Autistic had always made me feel separated from the rest of the population on Earth. I somehow found comfort in the fact that I had found a subject on objects away from our planet, a subject that I enjoyed and knew better than many of my bullies. Indeed, when younger I used to pretend to be a robot from outer space with hidden powers to eliminate the teasing from Earthlings.

The study of astronomy and outer space continues to fascinate me to this day, particularly the scale of the cosmos. On occasions, when I have had difficulty sleeping I have not resorted to counting sheep; instead I attempt to calculate how long it would take to reach various points in the universe travelling at different speeds. We shall examine some examples of these shortly, and I shall use my mathematical knowledge to estimate how long it would take a tortoise to walk from one end of a path to the other, when the length of that path is as great as the known universe. But first we need to ask another question. Exactly what is the universe? According to one definition the universe is everything that exists, has existed, or ever will exist. It contains everything from our own sun and solar system, including the Earth, right up to the furthest galaxy. But the more we think about it, the more unexplainable things become.

The modern scientific theory estimates that our universe came into being about 15,000 million years ago in a tremendous explosion called the Big Bang. Ever since then, matter (which later collected together under forces of gravity to form galaxies) has been sprawling outwards in all directions, with the overall universe expanding continuously. It's all very well saying this, but what happened before this Big Bang? If you remark that there was nothing, then surely a region of 'nothing' constitutes more empty space, and hence more universe. Or maybe there are an infinite number of unknown universes in addition to the one we know about. Perhaps our thinking of space being three-dimensional is too narrow minded. Just because we can't see or notice something doesn't mean it's not there; like a young child, whose early experience of Maths is that the counting numbers one, two, three and so on are the only numbers that exist, and does not learn until much later the concepts of negative numbers, fractions and zero.

There may be an infinite number of dimensions as well as an infinite number of universes. We could picture the scene in a world of say five dimensions where we are at the bottom of what seems to be a valley, yet no matter how much we attempt to climb, we appear to be getting no higher in relation to our surroundings. Aircraft could fly through the air one moment and then apparently disappear, just as in two-dimensional space one could view the front of the aircraft, this expanding as the middle passes through our point of reference, then the tall end, and then nothing again, since the plane would only be in one particular fixed third co-ordinate for an instant. In many of these alternative realities, time may not run at the same speed as we are accustomed to. What seems like millions of years to us may be only a few seconds elsewhere.

We can imagine a scenario where perhaps someone in a much larger universe than ours is doing the washing up. While they proceed, a single soap bubble is formed, expands and then rises through some alternative medium. This single bubble could represent our entire universe, and what to that being will seem like only a few seconds in the lifetime of a soap bubble before it pops will to us seem like thousands of millions of years. Objects such as the planets and stars that we have come to know about will represent only the tiniest particles in this much larger universe. In turn, perhaps every particle of microscopic size in our known universe represents a whole new universe on a vastly smaller scale, with its own stars, planets, life-forms and time speed of existence. Every particle in that universe could represent a still smaller universe, and so on for ever, an infinite hierarchy of universes, both up and down in scale. There is nothing we know about at present to say this isn't true. There are also an infinite number of other possibilities.

The concept of parallel universes is a particularly exciting one. Basically the idea is that if there are countless different universes then some of these are likely to be very much like our own, even in such details as having a man called Marc writing his autobiography about Autism! Perhaps everything is identical in one of these universes apart from having blue leaves on all the trees. We should also realise that not all these universes may be complete in their own right. They may exist within and around us. What seems to be real could be just a dream, while what appears to be a dream could be real. And there's always the ultimate question: why are we here at all? The more one thinks about these things, the more mindboggling and unanswerable they seem to get. At the risk of getting too spaced out with our discussion (here we go with my jokes again!), let us remain in our own known universe for the moment.

Before we start looking at various distances in the cosmos let us get a basic picture of what is out there. Nearest to the Earth is our own satellite, the moon, the only other body in the solar system that man has set foot on. The rest of the solar system consists of the other eight known planets, which have (apart from two) numerous satellites between them, a large collection of comets and various lumps of rock, including asteroids. The planets all revolve around the central star of the solar system, which is of course the sun. The sun may look very different from other stars, but only because it is so much closer. In fact the sun is just an ordinary star in cosmic terms, and a rather dwarf one at that. In recent years, astronomers have begun finding planets that revolve around stars other than the sun. Let us travel briefly past all the chief planets in our solar system and take a look at what we can observe. But first we should distinguish between planets and stars.

Planets are generally much smaller bodies than stars, and revolve around the star. In addition, stars are large gaseous bodies that emit their own light. In sharp contrast, planets rely on the parent star's rays to enable them to shine (mirrorlike). If the sun was suddenly snuffed out, none of the planets would be visible. Life on Earth is totally dependent on the sun, without which we would all be frozen solid. Travelling inwards from the Earth towards the sun, our nearest neighbouring world is Venus. Almost as big as our planet, it is permanently covered in cloud, beneath which is a furnace-like environment hotter than an oven, and an atmosphere of choking carbon dioxide where the greenhouse effect has run riot. The clouds act as a shield, trapping the heat from the sun. A more hostile place is hard to imagine. Further in and closest to the sun is the small planet Mercury, a ball of rock with virtually no atmosphere to protect the surface from boiling heat in daytime to freezing cold at night. Neither of these worlds has a satellite.

Travelling away from the sun, we come to the red planet, Mars. Only about half the size of the Earth, it attracts much attention in being the most Earth-like planet with a similar length day. However, the atmosphere is much too thin for humans to breathe and consists chiefly of carbon dioxide, and to date no conclusive evidence has been found of any kind of life there. Outside the path of Mars are numerous chunks of rock, some no bigger than a fist, others hundreds of miles across. These are known as the asteroids and most of them occupy the region between Mars and the next planet outwards, Jupiter. A few of these however have more exaggerated orbits around the sun, and may on occasions be captured by the gravitational effects of a nearby planet and hence start revolving around that instead. Mars, for instance, has two tiny moons, Phobos and Deimos, only a few miles across, and these are very possibly captured asteroids.

Jupiter, fifth planet in orbit from the sun, with its great red spot, is truly the giant of our solar system. Over 1000 earths could be encompassed within it. Its great red spot alone (a massive storm system in the Jovan atmosphere) is bigger than our own world. The planet is known to have about 20 moons and more may be discovered. Almost like a miniature solar system in its own right, four of these moons, Io, Ganymede, Callisto and Europa, are very large and comparable to the planet Mercury's size. The next planet outwards is Saturn, a slightly scaled down and calmer version of Jupiter, and famous for its spectacular rings, which consist of thousands of small particles and rocks which orbit Saturn. It is now known that four of the planets have rings, but none as complex or as fascinating to observe as those of Saturn. It is also known to have at least 20 satellites. Both Jupiter and Saturn are made chiefly of gas, and have no obvious solid surface.

These six planets (including the Earth) were the only ones known in ancient times, but more recently three more have been discovered in our solar system. Uranus and Neptune, seventh and eighth planets from the sun, were discovered in 1781 and 1846 respectively. Like Jupiter and Saturn, these worlds are made mainly of gas and have no solid surface. Though smaller than Jupiter and Saturn, they are still large worlds much bigger than the Earth and have about 30 moons between them. As a child, I was always curious about these two planets and used to dream about what they would look like close up. The chief reason for this was that before the *Voyager* probes visited them, very little was known about them and space books of that time often had detailed, lengthy chapters on the other planets and only a very brief one on these two.

The final planet, ninth in order from the sun, Pluto, was not discovered until 1930 and is still a bit of a mystery. It is very small, more like Mercury than the other outer planets, although much colder, and may very well be a stray asteroid. No spacecraft has ever viewed Pluto close up, and there won't be a craft anywhere near it for many years, although we know the planet has one satellite, Charon. In addition, our survey of the bodies of our local system would not be complete without a mention of the comets orbiting the sun, mainly beyond the orbit of Neptune. These are hazy looking bodies with centres resembling stars and tails which always point away from the sun. Some comets have such large orbits they take millions of years to circle the sun once, while others return to the inner solar system more often, including some famous ones such as Halley's Comet, which is seen from Earth once every 76 years.

On a much grander scale (we will see just how grand shortly) our local star, the sun, is just one of over 100,000 million stars in a vast spiral-shaped arrangement that we call a galaxy. Our galaxy is known as the Milky Way and it in turn is just one among millions of other galaxies of all shapes and sizes spreading across the depths of intergalactic space. The galaxies themselves are not spread evenly across the cosmos, but instead tend to form groups. The collection of galaxies that includes ours is known as the local group, containing about 30 members. There is some evidence that even these groups seem to collect together in still larger arrangements known as superclusters of galaxies. These superclusters spread as far away as observers can see. And the entire known universe is still expanding with all the groups of galaxies racing away from one another like spots on an expanding balloon.

The swiftest traveller we know is a ray of light. In just one second, light travels about 186,000 miles. This is quick enough to travel round the whole earth seven times – the vast oceans, the Sahara desert, the United States and Russia. Light can skip the distance between Earth and our satellite the moon in just over a second. The sun and the nearby planets of Mercury, Venus and Mars are all within about eight minutes' travel. The giant outer planets are far more spread out, however, but we would still take no longer travelling on a light beam than the average family holiday in England. Jupiter, the giant of the planets, lies at a little over half an hour away. Saturn, with its famous rings, will take just over an hour, and even Neptune, the outermost gas giant, can be reached within four hours. But once we leave the solar system the adventure really starts. We encounter scales of a grand magnitude, simply too big to imagine for most. Even the nearest star apart from the sun is about 100 million times further away than our own moon. This star is known as Proxima Centauri and is actually the faintest component of a triple star system named the Alpha/Proxima Centauri system.

In one year a ray of light can travel nearly 6 million million miles. This distance is known as a light year, and is one of the chief units for measuring distances in space. Normal measurements such as miles and kilometres used on Earth have very little meaning in outer space when the figures become so large. Light takes just over four years to get to Proxima Centauri. This is about 7000 times further away from the Earth than the furthest planet in our solar system, Pluto. Our whole Milky Way galaxy is about 25,000 times as wide as the distance between us and Proxima Centauri, and light would take over 100,000 years to travel from one side to the other. A return trip taking 200 millennia suddenly makes the speed of light seem not so fast after all.

But there's much more! The nearest large similar-shaped galaxy to our own is situated over two million light years away. Remote objects such as quasars (which may be the formation of galaxies) have been observed over 10,000 million light years away from us. When we observe these things through a telescope we are actually looking back in time. Even the planet Jupiter that we observe from Earth is not the Jupiter of the present, but the one of over half an hour ago, because its light has taken that long to reach us. If the nearest large galaxy to our own (known as Andromeda) was suddenly taken away, we would not know this until more than 2000 millennia in our future. I suspect that astronomy and the way it is done today will be rather out of date by then! The concept of time and time travel also fascinate me, as well as having had a fixation on keeping to time because of my Autism.

I would love to know what this exact place where I'm sitting now writing my book was like 353 and 687 years ago, and 50,231 years ago, and all the years in between! How about a million years ago? What would be the difference in the surroundings of this exact location in one million BC and two million BC? And what about 1000 million years ago? Don't think there would be any advanced Internet products available on the market then! And of course I would like to repeat all these years but in the future. I don't think our lifetimes are nearly long enough to do every-thing we want. On cosmic terms, our lifespan is less than the blink of an eyelid. The universe is certainly a large enough place to travel about in, even at the speed of light. And there's one problem with this. Einstein's theory of relativity does not permit any material object of our universe to travel at the speed of light. In one sense this seems logical. Let us examine why.

In order for the universe to be properly structured there must be a cosmic speed limit. Otherwise, any particle could destroy all others if it travelled fast enough and crashed into them. A single nail colliding with the Earth at 1000 million times the speed of light would almost certainly destroy it and reduce our world to a puff of smoke. There is also evidence that time itself slows as one approaches the speed of light, and that it would theoretically be possible for a spaceman to leave Earth and travel to the Andromeda galaxy and back again within his lifetime as far as his time reference is concerned. But upon his return he would find the Earth as it will be over four million years in the future, with everyone he once knew all long since dead. Mass also increases as we near the speed of light, and would become infinite when we obtain this speed, which makes it impossible, seemingly.

Possibly there may be other ways of getting round this problem. After all, it would have been 'seemingly impossible' 1000 years ago to watch a group of men land on the moon on television. Maybe there are wormholes (doorways) to other parts of the cosmos through black holes (regions of space that have collapsed in on themselves with a pull of gravity so strong that not even light can escape) which we could reach in an instant. There could be particles in an alternative universe that only travel faster than light while still not breaking the rule of not travelling exactly at light speed. Or maybe there is some fundamental flaw in our reasoning, perhaps by not noticing something that would be obvious to a more advanced civilisation, almost like our earlier example when we were thinking two-dimensionally and then suddenly discovered the third dimension.

Even if we could somehow find a way to break the theory and travel faster than light, our own universe is still a very big place. At a mere ten times the speed of light it would still take a million years to reach many of the nearby galaxies. Travelling a million times faster than the speed of light, we could reach Proxima Centauri in about two minutes, but travelling across the Milky Way galaxy would take many weeks and an 8000 year trip (eight millennia) would be necessary to reach a quasar 8000 million light years away. Maybe moving at a million times the speed of light is still much too slow! And travel times are about to get far more lengthy as we next consider some slower and more realistic speeds that material objects can reach. In particular, doing so will not flaw the basic laws of relativity!

The fastest craft ever constructed to date by the human race has been the *Voyager 2* probe, which flew past all four gas giant planets in our solar system, and in doing so increased our knowledge of the worlds more than at any other point in history. Very approximately, the craft is now travelling about one ten-thousandth of the speed of light, so will require over 40,000 years to reach Proxima Centauri. A little multiplication will reveal that it would take over 1000 million years for it to travel from one side of our galaxy to the other. It's a long time to wait. To reach the Andromeda galaxy would take more than 20,000 million years, but the known universe itself is no more than 15,000 million years old in some models. To reach a quasar 10,000 million light years away and then return to Earth (if there was time to do so before the world ends) would take in the order of 200 million million years. Better take plenty of chocolate and coffee with you!

The type of spacecraft in which astronauts went to the moon is rather slower than *Voyager*. It reached the moon in about three days, but would take nearly a million years to get to Proxima Centauri. To reach the Andromeda galaxy would take about 500,000 million years. But we are still dealing with very fast speeds in terms of everyday life on Earth. Suppose now we consider a sports car driving at a maximum speed of 160 mph without any rest periods. If there was an imaginary road leading to various places in the cosmos, this car would take about two months to get to the moon, but nearly 18 million years to reach Proxima Centauri, and roughly 9 million million years to get to Andromeda. If these sort of times are still not big enough, we shall make them even more impressive by considering the time it would take for an average healthy man to walk across the known universe, and then do the same with our tortoise.

An average, fully grown man walks at perhaps 3 mph and could walk the distance to our moon in about nine and a half years. He could walk to Pluto, the furthest planet in our solar system, in roughly 127,000 years. He would take about 940 million years to reach Proxima Centauri, and could walk across our Milky Way galaxy from one side to the other in approximately twenty three and a half million million years. Walking to that quasar 10,000 million light years away would take about twenty three and a half million million million years. Finally we consider our tortoise, and for simplicity let us assume that its average speed is 0.3 mph. If the edge of the observable universe is 15,000 million light years away, it would take our little four-legged friend about 353 million million million years to complete the trip. In comparison, our ray of light could travel round the Earth more than 75,000 million million million million times in that period!

These numbers certainly are big – or are they? After reading Appendix 4 on large numbers, we probably won't think so any more. But in a nutshell, it's the simple fact that the universe is stranger than we imagine that makes it so fascinating. The concept of infinite is a mind-boggling one if we try to think about it rationally, yet prospects of facing infinite ideas are very likely when you start considering the forma-tion of the known universe and everything else that isn't known out there. We shall be meeting some infinite ideas again shortly, but before we leave our discussion on astronomy there are one or two things remaining that are worth a mention.

There is always the question of whether other life-forms exist apart from ourselves in the cosmos. Some people use the argument that since there are so many stars in the universe (more than all the grains of sand of all the Earth's beaches) it would be overwhelmingly improbable that we are the only intelligent civilisation. But further reflection makes us realise that this deduction depends on how likely it is that life will actually arise, given that conditions are suitable for it. The building blocks of living things consisting of DNA are very complicated, and demanded a long sequence of events to occur for life to form in our own world. If the odds on all these things happening elsewhere are only one in a billion billion, then we may cancel out the prospects of life elsewhere generated by large numbers of stars, and conclude that we are alone.

Despite numerous claims of UFO sightings, there has been no con-clusive proof to date of extraterrestrial life. I do believe that there are forces at work in this universe beyond our understanding, and we should respect them and believe in fate – that everything happens for a valid reason. But maybe our level of understanding is insufficient at present in answering the question 'Are we alone?'. After all, there is no reason why alien life should look anything like us. Indeed, it may be so different that when we finally come across it we will be unable to recognise it. Or maybe extraterrestrials have visited us, but are not showing themselves by their own resolutions of not interfering with emerging civilisations. Alternatively, perhaps no one has found us yet. We have seen how big the cosmos is. It is credible that they have not looked in our region of the galaxy. Whatever the true situation, the continued uncertainty will continue to fascinate me.

As a final viewpoint on the subject, I also believe that our continued existence on this planet could very well depend upon further exploration of space. The current world population is simply too large and demands more of the planet's resources than it is able to give. Yet even our own solar system is 13,500 times as big as the distance between the Earth and the moon. All that is needed is the will and financial backing to set up permanently manned bases on the moon and Mars, perhaps hollow out some asteroids which would have enough internal volume to home millions of people. There is plenty of room in our solar system for an increasing human population in the billions, unlike our own small Earth, which must have an upper limit on how many can co-exist safely without stripping the planet dry of every goodness.

In any case, now it is time to move on. The appendix sections would not be complete without some mathematical insight, since this is my favourite subject. All the same, it's worth considering that there are a lot of people who do not enjoy the subject at all and they will have the option of skipping the following appendices. That is their choice. The important thing is that we give plenty of encouragement to those who do want to learn about it. I have seen some really good students in the past who have been put off the subject for life by one careless remark by an unthinking teacher. My advice is to learn from this and always focus on the positives while not dwelling on what seems impossibly difficult. Any new skill, however small, if learnt properly, is an achievement and can be used as the basis for further progress.

Large Numbers

W hat's the largest number you can think of? How about a million billion trillion? We have already been dealing with numbers that appeared to be very large in our study of astronomy. But this is all a matter of perspective. In this appendix, I shall be explaining about numbers that are so large that they probably belong in another universe! We will start off with some of the most massive well-known numbers by mathematicians, and then build on that. In order for us to make progress, it is necessary to introduce some scientific notation. It can be very cumbersome, for example, to write out 1000 million in full – here it is: 1,000,000,000 – so scientists use the notation of various powers to eliminate a large string of zeros. For simplicity, I shall restrict discussion here to positive integer powers (slightly more complicated definitions exist for other number powers). With this restriction in mind, a number raised to a power n is defined as the product of n such numbers. For example, 10 to the power of 2, which is also known as 10 squared, is equal to $10 \times 10 = 100$. Similarly, 10 to the power of 3, known as 10 cubed, is equal to $10 \times 10 \times 10 = 1000$. There is a special notation that is used for powers, as shown in the table below.

	Written as	Number of 10s to multiply together	Result
10 to the power 2	10^2	2	$10 \times 10 = 100$
10 to the power 3	10^3	3	$10 \times 10 \times 10 = 1,000$
10 to the power 4	10^4	4	$10 \times 10 \times 10 \times 10 = 10,000$
10 to the power 6	10^6	6	$10 \times 10 \times 10 \times 10 \times 10 \times 10 = 1,000,000$
10 to the power 10	10^{10}	10	$10 \times 10 \times 10 \times 10 \times 10 \times 10 \times 10 \times 10 \times 10 \times 10 = 10,000,000,000$
10 to the power n	10^n	n	one followed by n zeros

Notice how the power dictates the number of zeros in the above table. We also note that the first five examples are merely special cases of the last example replacing n with 2, 3, 4, 6 and 10 respectively. And of course, we do not have to restrict our starting number to be 10; for example, 9 to the fourth power can be easily calculated as $9 \times 9 \times 9 \times 9 = 6561$. With a little thought, it becomes obvious that we can very quickly write down some vast numbers with this sort of notation. How about 10 to the power of 100, that is a one followed by a hundred zeros. If you're wondering what that looks like in full, I shall write it down. Here we are:

10,000,000,000,000,000,000,000,000,000,000,000,000,000, 000,000,000,000,000,000,000,000,000,000,000,000,000, 000,000,000,000,000,000,000.

This fellow is quite well known amongst mathematicians, and is called a googol after a boy related to an American mathematician called Edward

Kasner. Thinking back to our earlier discussions, I wonder what will be exactly 'here' where I am writing this book, a googol years in the future. Yet we have not even scratched the surface yet of my idea of a really large number. Let us make one more step in expanding the magnitude of our numbers by introducing the googolplex.

A googolplex is defined as ten to the power of a googol, that is a one followed by a googol zeros. I will not attempt to write out this number in full for it certainly wouldn't fit into this book. Actually, things are a bit more serious than that. A piece of paper with all the zeros of a googolplex written clearly on it could not be squashed into the known universe! Compare this with the approximate 10^{80} elementary particles that make up the observable cosmos. A googolplex is perhaps as far as most mathematicians would want to proceed, arguing that this is a large number indeed. But I now invite us to proceed much further. In fact we have only just begun. In order to progress further, we need to understand two additional mathematical definitions, that of factorial, and that of a sequence.

Once again I shall, for simplicity, restrict the following definition to positive integer values of n. We define n factorial, written as $n!$, to be the product of all the counting numbers from 1 up to n. That is:

$$n! = n(n-1)(n-2)(n-3)\ldots 3 \times 2 \times 1 \text{ for } n = 1, 2, 3$$

So for example:

$$3! = 3 \times 2 \times 1 = 6$$

$$4! = 4 \times 3 \times 2 \times 1 = 24$$

$$7! = 7 \times 6 \times 5 \times 4 \times 3 \times 2 \times 1 = 5040 \text{ and so on}$$

(Note: in mathematics 0! is also defined as being equal to 1, but we need not be concerned about this in our discussion.)

We can define a particular factorial in terms of lower factorials. For instance, since:

$(n-1)(n-2)(n-3)\ldots 3 \times 2 \times 1 = (n-1)!$, by definition we must have

$$n! = n(n-1)!$$

Other deductions can easily be made, i.e.

$$\frac{n!}{(n-2)!} = \frac{n(n-1)(n-2)!}{(n-2)!} = n(n-1)$$

Thus to evaluate

$$\frac{100!}{98!}$$

We know the answer is $100 \times 99 = 9900$ without needing to work out the separate factorials.

The size of factorial numbers grows extremely rapidly. 20! is larger than 2×10^{18}, that is a two followed by 18 zeros. And 70! is larger than a googol, and 100,000! would be quite a handful for even a computer to work out.

I will now define what is meant by a sequence of numbers. This is an ordered set of numbers with a definite rule for working out each term. Consider the numbers

1, 2, 3, 4, 5, 6...

These are of course the counting numbers, but can be regarded as a sequence of which the first term is one, and with the rule each successive term can be found by adding one to the term preceding it. We often use the notation a_n to represent the *nth* term of a sequence. So in the example just given, $a_1 = 1, a_2 = 2, a_3 = 3$ etc., and $a_n = n$. This particular sequence is an infinite one (since there is no largest number, more on this shortly) but sequences in general can be either finite or infinite. The sequence {2, 4, 6, 8}, whose first term is 2, and each successive term is found by adding two to the preceding term, is an example of a finite sequence.

There are alternative ways of defining each term of a sequence. One of these is to use a general formula in terms of the *nth* term. Consider the sequence whose *nth* term is defined by the formula:

$$a_n = n^2 \text{ for } n = 1, 2, 3, 4, 5, 6$$

It follows that any particular term can now be calculated explicitly by substituting values for n into the general formula. So that $a_1 = 1^2 = 1$,

$a_2 = 2^2 = 4$, $a_3 = 3^2 = 9$, etc. Thus the full sequence, which is finite and contains six terms, can be written:

{1, 4, 9, 16, 25, 36}

Another way of defining a sequence is to do it inductively and express the nth term in terms of the $(n-1)th$ term, and the $(n-1)th$ term in terms of the $(n-2)th$ term, and so on. We need also to define what our starting term of the sequence, a_1, is in this case. Consider the sequence which has a first term of 2, i.e. $a_1 = 2$, and the nth term is defined in terms of the $(n-1)th$ term as follows:

$a_n = 3a_{n-1}$ for $n = 2, 3, 4, 5, 6, 7$

We first replace n by 2 in the general formula above to give:

$a_2 = 3a_1 = 3 \times 2 = 6$

Next, replacing n by 3 we have $a_3 = 3 \times 6 = 18$. We can repeat this process to obtain the rest of the terms of this sequence. We obtain:

{2, 6, 18, 54, 162, 486, 1458}

We could have defined this sequence in the alternative manner of giving the first term as 2 with the rule of getting each term by multiplying the preceding term by 3. But we shall use the inductive definition to define our real big mind-boggling numbers that we are about to approach. They will be based on the following idea. Let us define a sequence as follows:

$a_n = [(a_{n-1})!]^{[(a_{n-1})!]}$ for $n = 2, 3, \ldots$

where a_1 can take any selected value we choose. So, in order to calculate a particular term, we work out the factorial of the previous term, and then raise that number to the power of itself. First we will use a simple base number to illustrate the method. Then we will be in a position to define our majestic larger than life numbers. Let us see just how quickly the magnitude of each term of this sequence grows by choosing $a_1 = 2$. This is the smallest integer value for which the terms do grow, for if we had chosen $a_1 = 1$, then all terms of this sequence would be identically one.

Using the definition $a_2 = (2!)^{(2!)}$. Now $2! = 2$ thus $a_2 = 2^2 = 4$. This doesn't seem too big, does it? Looks can be deceptive! Let us iterate again. $a_3 = (4!)^{(4!)}$ Now $4! = 4 \times 3 \times 2 \times 1 = 24$, thus $a_3 = 24^{24}$, and this, using a calculator, comes to about 1.334×10^{33}, that is 1334 followed by 30 zeros, which is a very big number in everyday terms. Now the fun really starts if we wish to calculate the fourth term, a_4. Using the definition:

$$a_4 = (24^{24} \, !)^{(24^{24} \, !)}$$

and this number, my good friends, is getting large. We are now finally in a position to discuss the formation of the really mega-large numbers I have in mind. I shall again use the above sequence, but with a couple of differences. First, we need a much bigger starting value for a_1. After some careful thought, and noting how quickly the factorial function grows, I considered first the considerable size of a googolplex! and decided that for a_1 I would use this as the foundation of my iterations. I will define:

$$a_1 = (\text{googolplex!})^{(\text{googolplex!})} = A, \text{ say}$$

The above sequence as I have defined it is infinite, but let us make it finite by terminating the iterations when n reaches A in magnitude. That is we perform $A - 1$ iterations and calculate a_A. Let us now denote this massive result by $b_1 = B = a_A$ where B can now be used as the first term in a new sequence:

$$b_n = \left[(b_{n-1})! \right]^{[(b_{n-1})!]} \quad \text{for } n = 2, 3, 4 \ldots B$$

We now proceed as before with continued iterations until we reach b_B. There are a couple of important differences to this second sequence, for not only is the first term much bigger, but we are performing vastly more iterations, in fact $B - 1$ of them.

Now we let $b_B = c_1 = C$ where C is our starting term of a third sequence defined as:

$$c_n = \left[(c_{n-1})! \right]^{[(c_{n-1})!]} \quad \text{For } n = 2, 3, 4 \ldots C$$

We next calculate c_C. We then use this result as the starting value of $d_1 = D$ of a similar defined sequence and calculate d_D. We then continue this process right through the alphabet, obtaining 26 different sequences.

Each sequence is such that the basic rule of working out each term from the preceding one is the same, yet each successive sequence has a much greater starting value, and vastly more iterations then the preceding one. The first of my favourite large numbers is the value of z_z, that is the sequence number 26 defined in the above manner iterated $Z - 1$ times. Let us consider some properties of z_z.

In my view this is an extremely large number. But it's certainly still finite. There are bigger numbers, one of the simplest being $z_z + 1$. There is a marked difference between a finite and infinite quantity which always applies. For instance, although the following fact may make you gasp, it is mathematically true. The simple fact is that z_z is no closer to infinity than is the number one. For when we talk about infinite quantities, we are referring to something larger than any finite number, no matter how large.

For the mathematically interested, for the large numbers we are considering, taking M as a typical example, $M!$ is virtually equal to:

$$\sqrt{(2\pi)}\, e^{-M} M^{M + \frac{1}{2}}$$

This is called Stirling's formula.

Of course, there is no reason why we need stop at 26 or even 26! different increasing length sequences in the above manner described. Suppose we continued the above process a further googolplex! times. The end result, call it Marc's number if you wish, is still finite, and is still no closer to infinity than the number one. All the same, there is a certain fascination in creating numbers of this size, finite maybe, but large enough to bend your imagination backwards. I think you will agree that there are certainly some larger numbers than a million billion trillion around. Now may be a good time to bring these thoughts to an end, for there are a great many practical aspects of mathematics to help us with life's challenges, and ones in which size is not overwhelming!

Making Life Easy

I n this second appendix on Maths, I shall attempt to break down some apparently difficult problems into a set of smaller, easier ones, which is always a good way to proceed if one is not certain of things. You do not need a set of Maths degrees to fathom out many problems, and the examples I have chosen should be within most GCSE pupils' abilities to understand. It's often important to look at a problem in the right way, for I have seen many a student go 'off the beaten track' so to speak, and spend hours writing away when a short-cut trick of the trade method will get the solution in a few minutes. I am not ashamed to admit that it's happened to me on occasions as well. From a teacher's point of view, it is vital that one not only fully understands the problem, but is also aware of exactly how to communicate that knowledge to the students. Failure to do the latter could make it as difficult for the learner as Autistic people have trouble socialising, and we know about that now, don't we!

We shall be dealing with squares and square roots of numbers in our examples, and let us clarify the difference between these two things (a surprising number of people find this difficult). First, the *square* of a number, or second power, is defined as that number multiplied by itself. Thus, 7 squared, written as 7^2, is equal to $7 \times 7 = 49$. Similarly, 9 squared is $9^2 = 9 \times 9 = 81$, and 40 squared is $40 \times 40 = 1600$.

Now suppose I started with a certain number, squared that number to obtain a known answer. Then my starting number is a *square root* of the known answer. So, if I started with my number and found that when I squared that number I obtained 36, then what did I start with? Clearly 6 is an answer because $6 \times 6 = 36$. Upon reflection, it is not the only possibility, however, because by the rules of signs $(-6) \times (-6) = 36$ also, so that -6 is also a square root of 36. This is in fact generally true in that all real positive numbers have two square roots, equal in magnitude but of opposite signs. Thus because $10 \times 10 = 100$ and $(-10) \times (-10) = 100$, the square roots of 100 are 10 and -10, which is usually abbreviated as ± 10. Thus we can also state that the square of -10 and the square of 10 is 100. In general, if b is a real positive number, and $a \times a = b$ than a is a *square root* of b. Another way of saying this is that if the number b can be expressed in terms of two equal factors a, then a is a square root of b (a factor is a number that will divide exactly into the given number without remainder).

Consider now the equation $x^2 = 144$. Let us think what this equation tells us. It says that we start with an unknown number x, and when we multiply this number by itself we obtain the known answer of 144. So from the above discussion we know we need the square roots of 144, that is we wish to express 144 in terms of a multiplication of two equal factors. Since $12 \times 12 = 144$ and $(-12) \times (-12) = 144$, we see that ± 12 are the only possibilities for the square roots of 144. It follows that our number x must take one of these values. Hence the solutions of the above equation are:

$$x = \pm\sqrt{144} = \pm 12 \text{ (Note } \sqrt{x} \text{ denotes the positive square root of } x.)$$

Note how finding a square root is the reverse operation to finding the square, and by taking square roots of both sides of the above equation we eliminated the square sign of the unknown x.

Now consider an equation of the form:

$$\left(x - 5\right)^2 = 196$$

At first sight this looks rather difficult. The temptation for many students would be to expand out the bracket on the left-hand side and form a quadratic equation which they would have to remember, or refer to their textbook on how to find the solutions. But let us look at things from a different angle, and consider an easier situation. If the $x - 5$ expression just had *one* term, y say, then we would have the equation:

$$y^2 = 196$$

which is very like the previous equation that we solved by taking square roots of both sides. Here, since 14 is a factor of 196 and $196 = 14 \times 14 = (-14) \times (-14)$ we would know that:

$$y = \pm\sqrt{196} = \pm 14$$

But how can we link this to our original equation which has $(x - 5)^2$ instead of y^2 ? A little thought will reveal that we have already done the hard work. For if we let $y = x - 5$ and substitute this into our first equation we will obtain exactly the latter equation just solved. All we need do now is to substitute back to find the values of x:

If $y = 14$, then $14 = x - 5$, thus $x = 19$

If $y = -14$, then $-14 = x - 5$, thus $x = -9$

So the two solutions of the original equation are $x = -9$ and $x = 19$.

Now we look at the result of expanding brackets of the form:

$(a + b)(a - b)$ where a and b are any real numbers

By definition of expansion we must multiply every term in the first bracket by every term in the second bracket. Thus:

$$(a + b)(a - b) = a(a - b) + b(a - b)$$
$$= a^2 - ab + ab - b^2$$
$$= a^2 - b^2$$

We will now look at another example of something where there may be a temptation to proceed on a really long-winded solution which is not really necessary. Consider the problem of simplifying the expression:

$$(a - b + c - d)^2 - (a + b - c + d)^2$$

We could try to multiply this out, but both expressions combined would result in the order of 20 terms. We would probably make a tremendous mess and loads of mistakes. So instead, let us once again use our simplifying strategy. If things look complicated, try to make them easier. If e and f are real numbers we would know how to factorise $e^2 - f^2$ from the above expansion in reverse:

$$e^2 - f^2 = (e + f)(e - f).$$

So let us substitute $e = a - b + c - d$ and $f = a + b - c + d$. Then our problem reduces to the one line of factorising above. Since $e + f = 2a$ and $e - f = 2(c - b - d)$ the answer we require is:

$$4a(c - b - d)$$

Thus we have reduced a whole page of work to just two lines simply by looking at things in the right way, like sealing up the holes in our jug example on helping Autism correctly.

Remember that anything is possible if you put your mind to it, including in Maths. How about proving the quadratic formula for the solutions of quadratic equations? Ugh! Thousands of you students are now no doubt saying, 'It took me half of last year just to memorise this formula and use it, let alone prove where it comes from.' But did you think it was possible to ride a bike when you were six months old? Learning the derivation of the quadratic formula will be no more difficult for you today then learning to ride a bike for the first time was a few years back!

Let's begin with the definition of a quadratic equation. Its most general form is:

$$ax^2 + bx + c = 0$$

where a, b and c are constants, and a is non-zero. I shall restrict this discussion to a, b and c being real constants (they don't have to be, and often aren't at higher levels of Maths, but I haven't introduced non-real numbers so far!).

Our task is to obtain a formula for x in terms of the constants a, b and c. First, I will divide both sides of the equation by a. This is a perfectly legitimate move since a is non-zero. I obtain:

$$x^2 + \frac{bx}{a} + \frac{c}{a} = 0$$

I am now going to add the term

$$\frac{b^2}{4a^2}$$

to both sides, again a legitimate move, as long as I do the same to both sides. The reason for adding this term will become clear. I now have:

$$x^2 + \frac{bx}{a} + \frac{b^2}{4a^2} + \frac{c}{a} = \frac{b^2}{4a^2} \text{ or } x^2 + \frac{bx}{a} + \frac{b^2}{4a^2} = \frac{b^2}{4a^2} - \frac{c}{a}$$

transferring the

$$\frac{c}{a}$$

term to the right-hand side.

So far, you might argue, I seem to have, if anything, made our original equation more complicated by all this dividing and adding terms. But now we come to the clever bit which will vastly make things easier. Consider the expansion of:

$$\left(x + \frac{b}{2a}\right)^2$$

This by definition is:

$$\left(x + \frac{b}{2a}\right)\left(x + \frac{b}{2a}\right)$$

which by the rules is equal to:

$$x\left(x + \frac{b}{2a}\right) + \frac{b}{2a}\left(x + \frac{b}{2a}\right) = x^2 + \frac{bx}{2a} + \frac{bx}{2a} + \frac{b^2}{4a^2} = x^2 + \frac{bx}{a} + \frac{b^2}{4a^2}$$

This is precisely the left-hand side of our equation. We have thus done the hard work and are nearly there. We can write:

$$\left(x + \frac{b}{2a}\right)^2 = \frac{b^2}{4a^2} - \frac{c}{a}$$

We can tidy up the right-hand side of our equation a bit by expressing each part over a common denominator. Thus:

$$\left(x+\frac{b}{2a}\right)^2 = \frac{b^2-4ac}{4a^2}$$

Now by making a substitution for

$$\left(x+\frac{b}{2a}\right)$$

or by doing it mentally, using exactly the same technique as with the previous equations with squares, we take square roots of both sides to obtain:

$$x+\frac{b}{2a} = \frac{\pm\sqrt{(b^2-4ac)}}{2a}$$

Finally, subtracting

$$\frac{b}{2a}$$

from both sides we obtain the well-known (I hope!) formula:

$$x = \frac{-b\pm\sqrt{b^2-4ac}}{2a}$$

We have just accomplished a remarkable feat! We have now devised a way for solving not just one quadratic equation, but *any* in the above form. The process of adding our term

$$\frac{b^2}{4a^2}$$

to our equation to express the left-hand side as a perfect square is known as the method of 'completing the square' and can also be used to solve any quadratic equation of the above form, although the solutions will not be real numbers if b^2 is less in magnitude than $4ac$. We shall be looking at such a case shortly, and introducing the concept of a complex number.

But first let us look at a typical quadratic equation with real solutions. All we need do with the above formula is identify the values that a, b and c take and plug them in. Alternatively we can complete the square. Consider the quadratic equation:

$$3x^2 + 2x - 8 = 0$$

Comparing this with our general form:

$$ax^2 + bx - c = 0$$

we see that $a = 3$, $b = 2$ and $c = -8$ in this case. From this:

$$b^2 - 4ac = 2^2 - 4\,(3)(-8) = 4 + 96 = 100$$

Thus by substituting into the general expression for the solutions of x we obtain directly:

$$x = \frac{-2 \pm \sqrt{100}}{2(3)} \quad \text{and since } 100 = 10 \times 10,\ \sqrt{100} = 10$$

Thus:

$$x = \frac{-2 \pm 10}{6}$$

and the two possible solutions of the equation above are:

$$x = \frac{4}{3} \quad \text{and } x = -2$$

Alternatively, if we wished to use the method of completing the square, recall that first we require the coefficient of x^2 to be one; we can make this so by dividing both sides of the above equation by 3. We obtain:

$$x^2 + \frac{2x}{3} - \frac{8}{3} = 0$$

Now we note that since:

$$\left(x + \frac{1}{3}\right)^2 = x\left(x + \frac{1}{3}\right) + \frac{1}{3}\left(x + \frac{1}{3}\right) = x^2 + \frac{2x}{3} + \frac{1}{9}$$

We shall add $\frac{1}{9}$ to both sides which will make the left-hand side a perfect square. That is:

$$x^2 + \frac{2x}{3} + \frac{1}{9} - \frac{8}{3} = \frac{1}{9} \quad \text{or} \quad \left(x + \frac{1}{3}\right)^2 = \frac{25}{9}$$

Taking square roots of both sides with the usual method, we obtain:

$$\left(x + \frac{1}{3}\right) = \frac{\pm 5}{3} \quad \text{from which either } x = \frac{4}{3} \text{ or } x = -2 \text{ as before.}$$

Next we will introduce a new number i with the property that its square is equal to -1 (many engineers use j instead of i to avoid confusion with notation where i is used to stand for current). Thus according to our definition:

$$i^2 = -1$$

The number i is clearly not real, since no real number has a square of -1. Remember that a negative real number multiplied by itself gives a positive result. Noting also that $(-i)(-i) = +i^2 = -1$, we deduce that $-i$ is also a square root of -1, and thus the solutions of the equation:

$$x^2 + 1 = 0$$

are given by $x = \pm i$. The number i is known as an imaginary number, and we can express other square roots of negative real numbers in terms of i. For example:

$$\pm\sqrt{-64} = \pm\sqrt{64}\sqrt{-1} = \pm 8i$$

$$\pm\sqrt{-18} = \pm\sqrt{18}\sqrt{-1} = \pm\sqrt{2}\sqrt{9}i = \pm 3\sqrt{2}i$$

More generally, any number of the form $a + bi$ (where a and b are real numbers) is known as a complex number. It follows from this definition that all real numbers are a subset of all complex numbers where b takes the value zero.

This is rather like picturing all the numbers that you may have worked with so far as being placed on your worktable (the real plane), whereas all the complex numbers would fill your room (and more). Usually, when dealing with numbers in the above form where b is not zero we denote them by z, although w is sometimes used. Moreover, supposing we have two complex numbers:

$$z_1 = a_1 + b_1 i \text{ and } z_2 = a_2 + b_2 i$$

where a_1, a_2, b_1 and b_2 are all real numbers, and consider the difference:

$$z_1 - z_2 = (a_1 - a_2) + (b_1 - b_2)i$$

We observe from this that the only way that $z_1 = z_2$ will be if *both* $a_1 = a_2$ *and* $b_1 = b_2$. Thus although the above may look like one single equation, it actually generates two, namely by equating the coefficients of the real and imaginary parts.

Next, let us consider the following problem. What numbers have a square of i? That is, can we solve the complex equation $z^2 = i$? While there are quicker and perhaps slightly neater ways of solving this equation, the purpose of my method is to illustrate how we can deduce the answers using only the fairly elementary knowledge discussed already. We already know the general form of our answers, they will be represented by numbers of the type:

$$z = c + di \text{ where } c \text{ and } d \text{ are real numbers.}$$

Our task is to try and find the numerical possibilities for the values of c and d in this case. What we do know is that:

$$\left(c + di\right)^2 = i$$

but:

$$\left(c + di\right)^2 = \left(c + di\right)\left(c + di\right) = c\left(c + di\right) + di\left(c + di\right) = \left(c^2 - d^2\right) + 2cdi$$
since $i^2 = -1$

Now the only way that $c^2 - d^2 + 2cdi$ can equal i is if:

$$c^2 - d^2 = 0 \qquad\qquad (1)$$

$$2cd = 1 \qquad\qquad (2)$$

by comparing coefficients of real and imaginary parts. From equation (1) it follows that $c = \pm d$. If $c = -d$ then from

(2) $d^2 = \dfrac{-1}{2}$

and we have already seen that this has no real solutions. Since d is to be real we can neglect this possibility.

Thus $c = d$. Thus $d^2 = \dfrac{1}{2}$ from which $d = \dfrac{\pm 1}{\sqrt{2}}$.

By multiplying top and bottom of this fraction by $\sqrt{2}$ we will still have the same fraction. Applying this and substituting for c and d into our general solution form we deduce that the two solutions of our complex equation, and the two square roots of i, are given by:

$$z = \pm\left(\frac{\sqrt{2}}{2} + \frac{\sqrt{2}i}{2}\right)$$

Finally, we shall use our new-found knowledge to find the eighth roots of unity. That is we will solve the complex equation:

$$z^8 = 1$$

There are eight solutions here, two of them being real, the others are complex number solutions. This may seem an impossible task but it does not really require any new skills other than those that have already been discussed. Just a bit of ingenuity and we are well on the way to solving an equation at least eight times more complicated than a linear one. Let us use our usual procedure of breaking the problem down into a set of simple ones. For starters, we can subtract 1 from both sides of the equation.

If $z^8 = 1$, then $z^8 - 1 = 0$. Fair enough, but so far we do not seem to have made much progress. However, remembering the identity $a^2 - b^2 = (a + b)(a - b)$ and noting that $z^8 = (z^4)^2$ we realise that the left-hand side can be factorised to give:

$$\left(z^4 + 1\right)\left(z^4 - 1\right) = 0 \quad \text{(note that } a = z^4 \text{ and } b = 1\text{)}$$

The right-hand factor in the above expression can be factorised again to give:

$$\left(z^4+1\right)\left(z^2+1\right)\left(z^2-1\right)=0$$

One more crucial observation and we are halfway home. We have a set of three brackets whose product is zero. The only way this is possible is if one (or more) of the brackets on the left-hand side is zero. That is, if we let:

$$m=z^4+1 \quad n=z^2+1 \quad \text{and} \quad p=z^2-1$$

then:

$$mnp=0 \quad \text{will imply } m=0, \; n=0 \text{ or } p=0$$

But we already know the two solutions of $n=0$ to be $z=\pm i$ and the solutions of $p=0$ are fairly trivially $z=\pm 1$ (the two square roots of 1). Thus we have already obtained four of our solutions, and we need only now consider how to deal with the factor m. We apply a mathematical trick to this slightly less trivial factor to enable us to factorise further. Now:

$$\left(z^2+1\right)^2 = z^4+2z^2+1$$

This implies that:

$$z^4+1=\left(z^2+1\right)^2-2z^2$$

Now we can use our identity with $a=z^2+1$ and $b=2z^2$ to factorise. So:

$$m=0 \text{ implies } \left(z^2+\sqrt{2}z+1\right)\left(z^2-\sqrt{2}z+1\right)=0$$

Our task is now reduced to solving two quadratic equations, for again the only way the product of the two brackets above can be zero is if one of the brackets is zero. Despite the unknown being complex (z instead of x) the equations are still in standard form and we can use the usual quadratic formula for solution. For instance, from the left-hand bracket, comparing with the general form, we see that:

$$a=1, \; b=\sqrt{2} \text{ and } c=1$$

Thus:

$$b^2-4ac=2-4=-2$$

and:

$$\pm\sqrt{\left(b^2-4ac\right)}=\pm\sqrt{2}\sqrt{-1}=\pm\sqrt{2}i$$

and hence the two solutions of the equation:

$$z^2+\sqrt{2}z+1 \text{ are } z=\frac{-\sqrt{2}}{2}\pm\frac{\sqrt{2}i}{2}$$

Similarly, the two solutions of the other factor being equal to zero are:

$$z=\frac{\sqrt{2}}{2}\pm\frac{\sqrt{2}i}{2}$$

Thus, the eight complex numbers with the property that their eighth power is 1 are:

$$z_1=\frac{\sqrt{2}}{2}+\frac{\sqrt{2}i}{2}, \quad z_2=\frac{\sqrt{2}}{2}-\frac{\sqrt{2}i}{2},$$

$$z_3=-\frac{\sqrt{2}}{2}+\frac{\sqrt{2}i}{2}, \quad z_4=-\frac{\sqrt{2}}{2}-\frac{\sqrt{2}i}{2}$$

$$z_5=-i, \quad z_6=i, \quad z_7=-1 \text{ and } z_8=1$$

For all these numbers, $z\times z\times z\times z\times z\times z\times z\times z=1.$